Michigan State University
COLLEGE OF SOCIAL SCIENCE
DEPARTMENT OF ECONOMICS

Introduction to Macroeconomics
EC 202-001 and EC 202-002

Instructor: N. Obst

Selected Chapters from

Principles of Macroeconomics, Second Edition

Robert H. Frank   **Ben S. Bernanke**

Cornell University   *Princeton University*

– and –

Study Guide for use with Principles of Macroeconomics, Second Edition

Jack Mogah   **Bruce McClung**

– with –

Monetary Policy and the Equilibrium Price Level and Inflation Rate

Norman P. Obst
Michigan State University

 **Custom Publishing**

Boston   Burr Ridge, IL   Dubuque, IA   Madison, WI   New York   San Francisco
St. Louis   Bangkok   Bogotá   Caracas   Lisbon   London   Madrid   Mexico City
Milan   New Delhi   Seoul   Singapore   Sydney   Taipei   Toronto

The McGraw·Hill Companies

Introduction to Macroeconomics
EC 202-001 and EC 202-002

Norman P. Obst

Michigan State University
College of Social Science
Department of Economics

Selected Chapters from

Principles of Macroeconomics, Second Edition and

Study Guide for Use with Principles of Macroeconomics, Second Edition

with Monetary Policy and the Equilibrium Price Level and Inflation Rate

This book is a McGraw-Hill Custom Publishing textbook and contains select material from:
Principles of Macroeconomics, Second Edition by Robert H. Frank and Ben S. Bernanke. Copyright © 2004, 2001 by The McGraw-Hill Companies, Inc.
Study Guide for use with Principles of Macroeconomics, Second Edition prepared by Jack Mogah and Bruce McClung. Copyright © 2004 by The McGraw-Hill Companies, Inc.
Both are reprinted with permission of the publisher. Many custom published texts are modified versions or adaptations of our best-selling textbooks. Some adaptations are printed in black and white to keep prices at a minimum, while others are in color.
McGraw-Hill's Custom Publishing consists of products that are produced from camera-ready copy.
Peer review, class testing, and accuracy are primarily the responsibility of the author(s).

1 2 3 4 5 6 7 8 9 0 CDC CDC 0 9 8 7 6 5

ISBN 0-07-326916-6

Editor: Tamara Immell
Production Editor: Carrie Braun
Printer/Binder: C-DOC Services, Inc.

Study Guide

to accompany

Principles of Macroeconomics
Second Edition

by

Robert H. Frank
Ben S. Bernanke

Prepared by
Jack Mogab and Bruce McClung
Southwest Texas State University

To the Student

Welcome to the study of economics. We believe you will find the subject thoroughly intriguing. As you become an "economic naturalist" you will gain a clearer understanding of many important issues that currently may be perplexing to you. For example, what determines the cost of a car, or the salary you will earn when you graduate? Why does the economy experience booms and busts? How does the banking system create money? Why are federal deficits and surpluses so controversial?

These and many other topics are addressed in *Principles of Economics, Principles of Microeconomics,* and *Principles of Macroeconomics,* 2nd Editions by Robert H. Frank and Ben S. Bernanke, for which these Study Guides have been written. The Study Guide chapters parallel the chapters in the corresponding textbook, and each contains the following eight sections designed to assist your learning and to enhance your understanding of economics:

1. **Pretest.** This will test what you really know about the basic concepts and principles in the chapter and what you need to review before continuing on with more in-depth testing.
2. **Key Point Review.** The Learning Objectives for the chapter are listed to identify important concepts to master. The chapter's main ideas are summarized, and new terms are defined. **Hints** and **Notes** are provided to alert you to "tricks, clues and short-cuts".
3. **Self-Test: Key Terms**. All new terms are listed. Check your knowledge of key definitions by matching the term in the right-hand column with the appropriate definitions in the left-hand column.
4. **Self-Test: Multiple-Choice Questions.** Strengthen your grasp of the chapter material by choosing the correct answer from the alternatives for each question. Your ability to answer multiple-choice questions should serve as a good indicator of success on exams. You may wish to study for exams by reviewing these questions.
5. **Self-Test: Short Answer/Problems.** Here you will discover how the tools of economics can be applied to explore and clarify important issues. Problems are developed step by step. You are asked to analyze graphs and tables, to perform basic computations, and to select the best answers to a variety of fill-in statements.
6. **Economic Naturalist Applications.** Become an economic naturalist by applying the tools of economics to discuss these real-world issues with your classmates.
7. **Go To The Web.** This section will serve as a bridge between the Study Guide and the web-based E-Learning materials at http://www.mhhe.com/economics/frankbernanke2.
8. **Solutions**. Solutions, with explanations for the more complex and difficult items in the self-tests, are provided for the key-term, and multiple-choice questions, as well as for the short answer/problems.

The following suggestions will help make your study of economics successful:

Class Preparation or Must I Turn Off the TV?
It is essential that you prepare assignments BEFORE attending class so that you can understand the lecture and ask questions. Your instructor typically will not present all the materials in the text, but rather will concentrate on explaining the more complex ideas and applications.In preparing for class, first read the "Key Point Review" to identify the learning objectives for the chapter. Next, go to the chapter in the text. Read the "Summary," "Core Principles," and the "Key Terms" at the **end** of the chapter. Then, read the introductory section that will provide an overview of the topics to be covered in the chapter. The number

of topics will range from 4 to 7. Read and study one topic at a time, i.e., begin at the bold, upper-case red color heading and read until you get to the "Recap" box. Look for the paragraphs in the chapter that define and explain the concepts, principles, and laws related to that topic. These concepts, principles, and laws are listed at the end of each chapter as "Key Terms." As you read, mark these "terms" (as many as 3 to 5 per topic). You will notice that each topic can be presented in three modes--verbal, numerical (tables), and visual (graphs). This variety of presentation is important since economics is communicated through all three modes, and the test questions will reflect all three. After you have completed reading a topic, take a few minutes to read the Recap box. Verify that (1) you know (i.e. remember) the topic and important terms; (2) you understand (i.e. comprehend) that material; (3) you can relate the terms to one another when appropriate; and (4) you can relate the topic to the other topics in the chapter. Complete all the assigned topics in the above manner and write down any questions you have for the instructor.

Class Attendance or Why Not Go To the Rec Center?
Frankly, economics is such a demanding course that you will need all the help you can get. A great deal of that help comes from your instructor's lectures. The instructor's style and presentation will show you not only what the instructor considers to be important, but also how s/he approaches this subject. Getting notes from a friend will not give you this information. If you have followed the above suggestions in preparing for class, you will have some knowledge and understanding of the assigned topics. In class, the trick is to carefully combine four classroom skills - listening, taking notes, answering questions, and responding to questions. Listen with your mind. Be selective in what you write down. If you try to write everything that the instructor says, you will not have time to learn anything. For example, do not write a definition that has been given in the text. Listen for examples that differ from those in the text, special emphasis on a relationship between topics, and frequently repeated principles. Asking questions is the responsibility of the student. If you don't know enough to ask questions, you haven't done your job. If you have difficulty formulating questions during class, you should spend some time before class developing a list of questions you need to have answered. On the other side of the coin, you should also respond to the instructor's questions. You should not be shy about answering questions in class. An incorrect answer given in class is a free shot, while the same wrong answer on the test is very costly. The most effective way to use class time is to develop your ability to comprehend and apply economics concepts.

After Class or Do I Have To Do This Again?
Even if you have meticulously prepared for class and performed those four classroom behaviors, you still have a couple of things to do before you will be at the mastery level of the material. First, your class notes should be sketchy. You need to rewrite these notes in a more complete way before they get cold. Next, return to the Study Guide. Complete the three Self-Tests without referring to the text, and check your answers with the Solutions at the end of the Study Guide chapter. If your answers are correct, go onto the Economic Naturalist and the Go To The Web sections. If your answers to some of the questions are incorrect, go back and review the text and your class notes for those topics. Then return to the Study Guide Self-Tests to complete the questions you answered incorrectly (to further test your mastery of the material, go to the Electronic Learning Session in the Student Center at the Frank/Bernanke web site: http://www.mhhe.com/economics/ frankbernanke2). If you still do not understand the answers to the questions, either ask questions in the next class or go see your instructor for help.

If You Want To Learn It, Teach It.
To further test your comprehension of a topic, try explaining it in your own words to a classmate. Illustrate the idea with an example. If you can explain it clearly and give a good example, you have mastered the concept and its time to move on to the next chapter.

A Final Word
If the strategy outlined above seems like a lot of work, it is. You cannot achieve success in economics without hard work. It is estimated that the average student should spend 2-3 hours of quality study time for every hour spent in class.

Acknowledgments
It is a pleasure to acknowledge the assistance and support of Irwin McGraw-Hill in the preparation of this Study Guide. Particular thanks go to our capable and patient editors Tom Thompson and Paul Shensa.

Bruce McClung
Jack Mogab
June 2003

Contents

Chapter 4
Macroeconomics: The Bird's-Eye View of the Economy

I. Pretest: What Do You Really Know?

Circle the letter that corresponds to the best answer. (Answers appear immediately after the final question).

1. Macroeconomic policies are government policies designed to affect
   A. the legal system of the whole country.
   B. the performance of the economy as a whole.
   C. particular sectors of the economy.
   D. the environmental impact of all industries.
   E. the economic activity of the government.

2. Average labor productivity equals
   A. average production per year.
   B. total output.
   C. output per person.
   D. output per employed worker.
   E. production per person.

3. The value of output was $400 billion in Northland and $500 billion in Southland. The population of Northland was 80 million and the population of Southland was 90 million. There were 40 million employed workers in Northland and 80 million employed workers in Southland. Average labor productivity was higher in _____ and the standard of living was _____.

   A. Northland; the same in both countries
   B. Northland; higher in Southland
   C. Southland; higher in Northland
   D. Southland; higher in Southland
   E. Southland; the same in both countries

4. When jobs are hard to find, profits are low, few wage increases are given, and many companies go out of business, the economy is most likely in a(n)
   A. expansion.
   B. boom.
   C. recession.
   D. surplus.
   E. shortage.

5. The unemployment rate is the
   A. number of workers unemployed.
   B. number of workers in the labor force.
   C. number of workers minus those without a job.
   D. percentage of the labor force that is out of work.
   E. percentage of the population that is out of work.

6. The rate at which prices in general are increasing is called
   A. the inflation rate.
   B. the unemployment rate.
   C. average labor productivity.
   D. the standard of living.
   E. the trade balance.

7. A trade deficit occurs when
   A. government spending exceeds government revenue.
   B. government revenue exceeds government spending.
   C. exports equal imports.
   D. exports exceed imports.
   E. exports are less than imports.

8. Monetary policy refers to
   A. decisions to determine the federal budget.
   B. policy directed toward increasing exports and reducing imports.
   C. the determination of the nation's money supply.
   D. policies to reduce the power of unions and monopolies.
   E. policies aimed at changing the underlying structure or institutions of the economy.

9. _____ analysis addresses the question of whether a policy should be used, while _____ analysis addresses the economic consequences of a particular policy.
   A. Normative; positive
   B. Positive; normative
   C. Structural; monetary
   D. Monetary; fiscal
   E. Fiscal; monetary

10. Which of the following statements is positive?
   A. When the Federal Reserve increases the money supply, interest rates decrease.
   B. Large budget deficits should be avoided.
   C. Higher taxes are needed to support education.
   D. A tax cut that benefits low-income households is acceptable.
   E. The Federal Reserve should increase interest rates to slow down the economy.

Solutions and Feedback to Pretest
For each question you incorrectly answered, we strongly recommend taking the time to review the appropriate material before continuing. In the table below, the relevant textbook pages are listed for each question as well as the pertinent Learning Objective from the following Key Point Review.

Correct Answer	Textbook Page Numbers	Learning Objective
1. B	p. 99	7
2. D	p. 101	2
3. B	pp. 99-101	1
4. C	p. 102	3
5. D	pp. 102-3	4
6. A	p. 104	5
7. E	p. 104	6
8. C	p. 106	7
9. A	p. 107	8
10. A	p. 107	8

II. Key Point Review

This chapter introduces the subject matter of macroeconomics and the issues that are central to macroeconomics, as well as the basic tools of macroeconomics. Macroeconomics is the study of the performance of national economies and the policies governments use to try to improve that performance.

Learning Objective 1: Explain economic growth and standard of living.
Among the issues macroeconomists study are the sources of long-run economic growth and living standards. By standard of living, economists mean the degree to which people have access to goods and services that make their lives easier, healthier, safer, and more enjoyable. People with a higher standard of living have more goods to consume, but even the wealthiest people are subject to the principle of scarcity. Standard of living is inextricably linked to economic growth because the more we produce, the more we can consume. The high standard of living that Americans currently enjoy, for example, is the result of several centuries of economic growth in the U.S. Economic growth is a process of increasing the quantity and quality of goods and services that an economy can produce. Two questions

economist try to answer are, What causes economic growth to fluctuate over time? and Why does economic growth and the standard of living vary among countries?

Learning Objective 2: Calculate output per person and average labor productivity.
One factor related to economic growth is the growth in population and hence the number of workers available to produce goods and services. Increases in population allow the total output of goods and services to increase, but because the goods and services must be shared among a larger population it does not necessarily equate to a higher standard of living. Because of changes in population over time, output per person (total output divided by the number of people in an economy) is a much better indicator of living standards than total output. Macroeconomists also study the relationship between average labor productivity, or total output divided by the number of employed workers, and living standards. Because of the connection between production and consumption, average labor productivity is closely related to output per person and living standards.

Learning Objective 3: Define recession, depression, expansion and boom.
Economies do not always grow steadily; they go through periods of strength and weakness. Periods of rapid economic growth are called expansions, and when an expansion is particularly strong it is called a boom. Slowdowns in economic growth are called recessions, and particularly severe slowdowns (for example, during the 1930s) are referred to as depressions.

Note: There is no consensus among economists as to specific rates of economic growth that determine when an expansion should be called a boom, nor when a recession should be considered a depression. The difference between expansion and boom, and recession and depression is more qualitative than quantitative.

Learning Objective 4: Define unemployment rate and explain its relationship to recessions and expansions.
Fluctuations in the rate of economic growth cause changes in the unemployment rate, the fraction of people who would like to be employed but can't find work. Unemployment tends to rise during recessions and fall during expansions. But even during the "good times" some people are unemployed. Questions that macroeconomists try to answer include, why unemployment rises during periods of recession; why there are always unemployed people, even when the economy is booming; and why unemployment rates sometimes differ markedly from country to country.

Learning Objective 5: Define inflation and explain why macroeconomists study it.
Inflation is another important macroeconomic variable. Inflation is the rate at which prices in general are increasing over time. Inflation imposes a variety of costs on the economy and, thus, macroeconomists are interested in understanding the causes of inflation. Two questions that macroeconomists try to answers are why the rate of inflation varies from one period to

another, and what causes the rate of inflation to differ markedly from country to country. Inflation and unemployment are often linked in policy discussions because it is often argued that unemployment can only be reduced if the inflation rate is allowed to rise. Macroeconomists have studied this issue to provide a better understanding of this policy debate.

Note: Inflation does **not** imply that all prices are rising. The prices of some goods will be rising, but the prices of other goods may be falling, while the prices of a third group of goods may be constant. You can think of inflation as essentially an increase in the average price of goods and services.

Learning Objective 6: Define trade deficit and trade surplus.
While macroeconomics focuses on national economies, they recognize that national economies do not exist in isolation. They are increasingly interdependent. The international flows of goods and services are both an economic issue and a political issue. Trade imbalances, which occur when the quantity of goods and services that a country sells abroad (its exports) differ significantly from the quantity of goods and services its citizens buy from abroad (its imports), often cause economic and political problems. When a nation exports more than it imports, it runs a trade surplus, while the reverse results in a trade deficit. Macroeconomists try to determine the causes of trade surpluses and deficits and determine whether they are harmful or helpful.

Note: Because one country's exports are another country's imports, a trade surplus for one country implies a trade deficit for at least one other country.

Learning Objective 7: Identify the three types of macroeconomics policy: monetary, fiscal and structural policy.
In addition to analyzing the factors that affect the performance of the national economies, macroeconomists also study macroeconomic policy. Understanding the effects of various policies and helping government officials develop better policies are important objectives of macroeconomics. There are three major types of macroeconomic policy: monetary policy, fiscal policy, and structural policy. Monetary policy refers to the determination of the nation's money supply. In virtually all countries monetary policy is controlled by the central bank. Fiscal policy refers to decisions that determine the government's budget, including the amount and composition of government expenditures and government revenues. When government expenditures are greater than government revenues, the government runs a deficit, and when government revenues are greater than government expenditures, the government runs a surplus. The term structural policy includes government policies aimed at changing the underlying structure, or institutions, of the nation's economy.

Learning Objective 8: Explain the importance of normative and positive analyses.
Macroeconomists are often called upon to analyze the effects of a proposed policy. An objective analysis aimed at determining only the economic consequences of a particular policy is called positive analysis, while a normative analysis includes recommendations on whether a particular policy should be implemented. Positive analysis is objective and scientific, but normative analysis involves the values of the person or organization doing the analysis. Economists generally agree on issues related to positive analysis, but often disagree on normative analysis.

Learning Objective 9: Define aggregation and identify the strengths and weaknesses of aggregation.
Although macroeconomics takes a "bird's eye" view of the economy and microeconomics works at the ground level, the basic tools of analysis are much the same. Economists apply the same core principles in their efforts to understand and predict economic behavior. Because the national economy is much bigger, however, macroeconomists use aggregation to link individual behavior to national economic performance. **Aggregation** is the adding up of individual economic variables to obtain economy-wide totals.

Note: While macroeconomists and microeconomists employ the same basic tools of analysis, it does not always follow that the conclusions of macroeconomic analyses are the same as those of microeconomic analyses. An analogy: if an individual stands up at a football game, s/he can see better. If all spectators stand up, no one can see better.

III. Self-Test

Key Terms
Match the term in the right-hand column with the appropriate definitions in the left-hand column by placing the letter of the term in the blank in front of its definition. (Answers are given at the end of the chapter.)

1. _____ Decisions that determine the government's budget, including the amount and composition of government expenditures and government revenues

    a. aggregation

2. _____ Output per employed worker

    b. average labor productivity

3. _____ Addresses the consequences of a particular event or policy, not whether those consequences are desirable

    c. fiscal policy

4. _____ The adding up of individual economic variables to obtain economy-wide totals

    d. macroeconomic policies

5. _____ Determines the nation's money supply

    e. monetary policy

6. _____ Addresses the question of whether a policy should be used; involves the values of the person doing the analysis

    f. normative analysis

7. _____ Government actions designed to affect the performance of the economy as a whole

    g. positive analysis

8. ____ Government policies aimed at changing the underlying   h. structural policy
structure, or institutions, of the nation's economy

Multiple-Choice Questions
Circle the letter that corresponds to the best answer. (Answers are given at the end of the chapter.)

1. Economic growth is defined as a process of
   A. steady increase in the price of goods and services produced in the economy.
   B. steady increase in the quantity and quality of goods and services the economy can produce.
   C. constant increase in the quantity and quality of goods and services the economy can produce.
   D. constant increase in the price and quality of goods and services the economy can produce.
   E. constant increase in the number of jobs needed to produce the goods and service in the economy.

2. Our standard of living is directly tied to economic growth because
   A. everyone in society shares equally in the fruits of economic growth.
   B. the two terms are synonymous.
   C. in most cases economic growth brings an improvement in the average person's standard of living.
   D. the government can only improve people's standard of living if the economy is growing.
   E. a higher standard of living causes an increase in economic growth.

3. Microland has a population of 50 people and 40 of them worked last year with a total output of $200,000. The average labor productivity of Microland equaled
   A. $200,000.
   B. $200.
   C. $4,000.
   D. $40,000.
   E. $5,000.

4. During the 1930s, economies around the world were in a(n)
   A. recession.
   B. depression.
   C. expansion.
   D. boom.
   E. aggregation.

5. The unemployment rate is the
   A. percentage of people who would like to be employed but can't find work.
   B. number of people who would like to be employed but can't find work.
   C. fraction of people who are not working.
   D. number of people who are not working.
   E. number of unemployed people.

6. The unemployment rate increases during
   A. expansions and booms.
   B. expansions and recessions.
   C. booms and recessions.
   D. recessions and depressions.
   E. booms and depressions.

7. The inflation rate
   A. was higher in the 1990s than during the 1970s.
   B. increases the standard of living for people on fixed incomes.
   C. is the rate at which prices in general are increasing over time.
   D. is roughly equal in most countries.
   E. rises during recessions along with the unemployment rate.

8. If a country imports more than it exports, it has
   A. a trade balance.
   B. a trade deficit.
   C. a trade surplus.
   D. a budget deficit.
   E. inflation.

9. Government policies that affect the performance of the economy as a whole are called
   A. positive analysis.
   B. normative analysis.
   C. aggregation.
   D. microeconomic policy.
   E. macroeconomic policy.

10. Monetary policy
    A. refers to decisions that determine the government's budget.
    B. is controlled by a government institution called the Congressional Budget Office.
    C. is aimed at changing the underlying structure, or institutions, of the nation's economy.
    D. refers to the determination of the nation's money supply.
    E. can result in a budget deficit or a budget surplus.

11. The amount and composition of government expenditures and government revenues is determined by
    A. fiscal policy.
    B. monetary policy.
    C. structural policy.
    D. normative analysis.
    E. positive analysis.

-12. When a government collects more in taxes than it spends , it runs a(n)
   A. trade deficit.
   B. trade surplus.
   C. budget deficit.
   D. budget surplus.
   E. trade imbalance.

- 13. Supporters of structural policy argue that economic growth can be stimulated and living standards improved if
   A. the money supply is controlled by the central bank.
   B. the underlying structure, or institutions, of a nation's economy are changed.
   C. positive analysis is used to determine macroeconomic policy.
   D. normative analysis is used to determine macroeconomic policy.
   E. the federal budget is balanced.

-14. Normative analysis differs from positive analysis in that
   A. normative analysis is limited to determining the consequences of a particular policy, while positive analysis includes recommendations on the desirability of the policy.
   B. positive analysis is limited to determining the consequences of a particular policy, while normative analysis includes recommendations on the desirability of the policy.
   C. normative analysis is supposed to be objective and scientific, while positive analysis involves the values of the person or organization doing the analysis.
   D. economists typically agree on normative analysis, but often disagree on positive analysis.
   E. liberal economists use positive analysis, while conservative economists use normative analysis.

- 15. When macroeconomists add together the purchases of houses, cars, food, clothing, entertainment, and other goods and services by households in an economy, they are using
   A. normative analysis.
   B. positive analysis.
   C. aggregation.
   D. macroeconomic policy.
   E. fiscal policy.

 16. The strength of aggregation is that it helps to reveal the "big picture," but it's weakness is that it
   A. adds together "apples and oranges."
   B. involves the values of the person doing the analysis.
   C. gives excessive importance to the details.
   D. adds together data on different individuals.
   E. may obscure important details.

-17. Microland has a population of 50 people and 40 of them worked last year with a total output of $200,000. The output per person of Microland equaled
   A. $200,000.
   B. $200.

C. $4,000.
D. $40,000.
E. $5,000.

18. If Macroland sells more goods to foreign buyers than it purchases from them, it will have a
   A. trade balance.
   B. trade deficit.
   C. trade surplus.
   D. budget deficit.
   E. budget surplus.

19. When a government's expenditures are greater than its revenues, it has a
   A. budget deficit.
   B. budget surplus.
   C. trade deficit.
   D. trade surplus.
   E. trade imbalance.

20. In debating a government program for agriculture, Senator Agus from Kansas stated that spending should be increased because many farmers have suffered crop losses in the last year. Senator Scrimp from New York replied that his analysis indicates that an increase in spending for the program will increase the budget deficit. Senator Agus' statement is based on
   A. aggregation, while Senator Scrimp's statement is based on disaggregation.
   B. disaggregation, while Senator Scrimp's statement is based on aggregation.
   C. positive analysis, while Senator Scrimp's statement is based on normative analysis.
   D. normative analysis, while Senator Scrimp's statement is based on positive analysis.
   E. positive analysis, as is the statement of Senator Scrimp.

Short Answer Problems
(Answers and solutions are given at the end of the chapter.)

1. Economic Growth and Standard of Living
Use the data in the following table on output, employment, and population in the United States and Canada during 2002 to answer the questions below.

Economic variable	United States	Canada
Output (GDP)	$10,082,000,000,000	$875,000,000,000
Population	280,562,489	31,902,268
Employed persons	134,149,000	15,600,000

A. Output per person in the United States during 2002 equaled _____ and in Canada equaled _____ .
B. The average labor productivity in the United States during 2002 equaled _____ and in Canada equaled _____ .

C. Based on the data in the table above, which country had the highest standard of living during 2002? _____

2. Normative and Positive Analysis

In the blank following each statement, write an N if the statement is based on normative analysis, or a P if the statement is based on positive analysis.

A. The U.S. Energy Department stated that "increased production of oil in April and May 2000 will result in lower gasoline prices in the summer of 2000." _____

B. Alan Greenspan, Chairman of the Board of Governors of the Federal Reserve System, stated in March 2000 that "stock prices should rise no faster than household income." _____

C. In April 2000, William Sullivan, chief economist at Morgan Stanley Dean Witter, stated, "the retrenchment in equity [stock] prices will undoubtedly affect the economy later in the year." _____

D. On April 4, 2000 in an article published in *The Wall Street Journal*, Brian Blackstone and Jonathan Nicholson wrote, "The National Association of Purchasing Management monthly index, a broad measure of the health of the manufacturing sector, slipped a bit to 55.8 in March from 56.9 in February. That corresponds to a 4.8% annualized growth in gross domestic product." _____

E. In an article published on the Dismal Science web site, entitled, "Krugman vs. Republican Gas Tax Relief," Michael Boldin analyzed a tax policy proposed by the Republican Party congressional leaders. He states, "the Republican plan to immediately repeal the 4.3 cents per gallon federal surcharge that was added in 1993 and suspend the larger 18.4 cents per gallon federal tax if gasoline hits $2 per gallon is both untimely and unwise as a basic policy. For one it would hurt the highway fund that is a direct beneficiary of the tax. Worse yet, it would encourage gas consumption at a time when OPEC is keeping to a tight supply schedule and domestic inventories are dwindling." _____

F. In response to the question, what is the best Fed monetary policy course at this time (March 2000), Kevin Hassett, Resident Scholar at the American Enterprise Institute, responded, "The best Fed move right now would be no move, but it is a close call." _____

G. In an article published on the Dismal Science web site, entitled, "The New Economy's Dark Side," Mark Zandi states, "Families in the top 20% of the wealth distribution own well over 80% of the nation's wealth, while the top 5% of families own 60% of the wealth."

_____

3. Aggregation

Use the data in the following table on production in Macrolandia to answer the questions below.

Product	Price per unit	Units produced in 2002	Units produced in 2003
Clothing	$5	1000	600
Food	$2	5000	4000
Houses	$100	25	80

A. The total value of Macrolandia's output in 2002 equaled _____ and in 2003 equaled
    _____

B. Based on your answer to Question 3A, in 2003 Macrolandia produced (more/less)
    _____ output than in 2002.

C. The change in output from 2002 to 2003 would suggest the Macrolandia economy
    experienced _____ and, thus, one could deduce that the Macrolandian
    standard of living had (improved/worsened) _____ .

D. The workers of Macrolandia are equally divided into three groups who each specialize in
    producing a single good (i.e., clothing, food, or houses). Calculate the output produced by
    each group in 2002 and 2003. The clothing workers produced _____ output in 2002 and
    _____ in 2003, the food workers produced _____ output in 2002 and _____ in
    2003, and the housing workers produced _____ output in 2002 and _____ in 2003.

E. Thus, the output and standard of living of the (clothing/food/housing) _____
    workers of Macrolandia's increased, while the output and standard of living of
    (clothing/food/housing) _____ and (clothing/food/housing)
    _____ workers of Macrolandia's decreased .

F. Thus, the aggregation in Question 3A obscures the fact that a majority of Macrolandia
    workers output and standard of living (decreased/increased) _____ in 2003
    compared to 2002.

IV. Economic Naturalist Application
{No Economic Naturalist examples in this chapter}

V. Go to the Web: Graphing Exercises Using Interactive Graphs

This chapter provides you with an overview of *macroeconomics*, the study of the
performance of national economies and the policies governments use to try to improve
that performance. To help familiarize you with the *data* that macroeconomists use to
describe and analyze the health of the economy, please go to the Electronic Learning
Session in the Student Center at the Frank/Bernanke web site:
http://www.mhhe.com/economics/frankbernank2. The exercises there will provide you
with a "birds-eye" view of the economy and to help you notice *patterns* in
macroeconomic data and *describe* the historical behavior of the economy.

VI. Self-Test Solutions

Key Terms
1. c
2. b
3. g
4. a
5. e
6. f
7. d
8. h

Multiple-Choice Questions
1. B
2. C
3. E Average labor productivity = output/number of employed workers, (i.e., $200,000/40 = $5,000)
4. B
5. A
6. D
7. C
8. B
9. E
10. D
11. A
12. D
13. B
14. B
15. C
16. E
17. C Output per person = output/number of people in the economy, (i.e., $200,000/50 = $4,000)
18. C
19. A
20. D Senator Agus' statement refers to the desirability of the policy, while Senator Shrimps' statement only refers to the effect of the policy on the government's budget.

Short Answer Problems

1.
A. Output per person = Output divided by population $35,934.95; $27,427.52
B. Average labor productivity = Output divided by the number of employed persons $75,155.24; $56,089.74
C. The United States has the highest standard of living because both output per person and average labor productivity are higher than in Canada.

2.
A. P because the analysis is a prediction based on an application of the supply and demand model.
B. N because the analysis is based on his values (key word is "should")
C. P because the analysis is a statement of the effect of the change in stock market prices on the economy
D. P because it only indicates the statistical analysis
E. N because it is a statement of the desirability of the policy based on his values
F. N because it is a statement of the desirability of the policy based on his values
G. P because it only indicates the statistical findings of the economic analysis

3.
A. $(1,000 \times \$5) + (5,000 \times \$2) + (25 \times \$100) = \$17,500$; $(600 \times \$5) + (4,000 \times \$2) + (80 \times \$100) = \$19,000$
B. more
C. economic growth; improved
D. $1,000 \times \$5 = \$5,000$; $600 \times \$5 = \$3,000$; $5,000 \times \$2 = \$10,000$; $4,000 \times \$2 = \$8,000$; $25 \times \$100 = \$2,500$; $80 \times \$100 = \$8,000$
E. housing; clothing; food
F. decreased

Chapter 5
Measuring Economic Activity:
GDP and Unemployment

I. Pretest: What Do You Really Know?

Circle the letter that corresponds to the best answer. (Answers appear immediately after the final question).

1. Gross domestic product (GDP) equals the _____ of final _____ produced within a country during a given period of time.
   A. market value; goods
   B. market value; services
   C. market value; goods and services
   D. quantity; goods
   E. quantity; goods and services

2. Three equivalent ways to measure GDP are total _____, total _____, and total _____.
   A. profits; production; saving.
   B. expenditure; income; profits
   C. investment; consumption; saving
   D. production; income; expenditure
   E. revenue; profits; production

3. If Bountiful Orchard grows $200,000 worth of peaches, sells $50,000 worth of peaches to consumers and uses to rest to make jam that is sold to consumers for $200,000, Bountiful Orchard's contribution to GDP is
   A. $50,000.
   B. $100,000.
   C. $200,000.
   D. $250,000.
   E. $450,000.

4. Goods and services that are used up in the production of other goods and services are called
   _____ goods and services.
   A. intermediate
   B. final
   C. value added
   D. nominal
   E. real

5. Capital goods are treated as _____ goods and, therefore, _____ GDP.
   A. final; included in
   B. final; excluded from
   C. intermediate; included in
   D. intermediate; excluded from
   E. non-market; excluded from

6. Suppose a jar of DeLux popcorn that is ultimately sold to a customer at Friendly Groceries is
   produced by the following production process:

Name of Company	Revenues	Cost of Purchased Inputs
Fulton Family Farm	$1.00	0
DeLux Popcorn Co.	$2.50	$1.00
Friendly Groceries	$5.00	$2.50

   What is the value added by Friendly Groceries?
   A. $1.00
   B. $2.50
   C. $5.00
   D. $7.50
   E. $8.50

7. Given the following data for an economy, compute the value of GDP.

Consumption expenditures	1,500
Imports	500
Government purchases of goods and services	800
Construction of new homes and apartments	600
Sales of existing homes and apartments	500
Exports	400
Government payments to retirees	300
Household purchases of durable goods	400
Beginning-of-year inventory of stocks	600
End-of-year inventory of stocks	700
Business fixed investment	400

   A. 2,800
   B. 2,900

C. 3,300
D. 3,400
E. 6,700

8. Consumption spending includes spending on
   A. durables, nondurables, and services.
   B. stocks, bonds, and other financial instruments.
   C. capital goods, residential housing, and changes in inventories.
   D. goods and services by federal, state, and local governments.
   E. goods and services sold abroad minus goods and services produced abroad.

9. Which of the following would increase the investment component of U.S. GDP?
   A. You purchase a vacation at Disney World in Florida.
   B. You purchase shares of Disney stock.
   C. Disney World purchases tires for the monorail from a firm in Ohio.
   D. A French man purchases a vacation at a Disney theme park in France.
   E. A French child purchases mouse ears made in California at a Disney theme park in France.

10. Which of the following would increase the government purchases component of U.S. GDP?
    A. The U.S. federal government pays $3 billion in pensions to government workers.
    B. The U.S. federal government pays $3 billion in interest on the national debt.
    C. The U.S. federal government pays $3 billion in salaries to soldiers in the military.
    D. The U.S. federal government pays $3 billion in interest to foreign holders of U.S. government bonds.
    E. The U.S. federal government pays $3 billion to social security recipients.

Solutions and Feedback to Pretest
For each question you incorrectly answered, we strongly recommend taking the time to review the appropriate material before continuing. In the table below, the relevant textbook pages are listed for each question as well as the pertinent Learning Objective from the following Key Point Review.

Correct Answer	Textbook Page Numbers	Learning Objective
1. C	p. 111	1
2. D	pp. 110 - 21	2
3. D	pp. 114 - 16	2
4. A	p. 114	2
5. A	p. 114	2
6. C B	pp. 115- 16	2
7. C	pp. 117 - 20	2
8. A	p. 118	2
9. C	p. 118 - 19	2
10. D C	p. 119	2

II. Key Point Review

Economists depend on economic data to make accurate diagnoses; political leaders and policymakers also need economic data to help them in their decisions and planning. This chapter explains how economists measure two basic macroeconomic variables, gross domestic product (GDP) and the rate of unemployment. It also discusses how the measures are used, and provides some insight into the debates over the accuracy of the measures.

Learning Objective 1: Define GDP.

The **gross domestic product (GDP)** is the market value of the final goods and services produced in a country during a given period. To calculate GDP, economists aggregate, or add up, the market values of the different goods and services the economy produces. Economists, however, do not include the value of all goods and services in the calculation. Only the market values of **final goods and services**, the goods or services consumed by the ultimate user, are counted as part of GDP. The market values of **intermediate goods and services**, those used up in the production of final goods and services, are not included when calculating GDP because they are already included in the market value of the final goods and services.

Note: The distinction between final and intermediate goods is difficult to determine for some goods, e.g., capital goods. **Capital goods** are long-lived goods that are used to produce other goods and, thus, are not exactly final goods but neither are they intermediate goods. To overcome this difficulty, economists have conventionally classified newly-produced capital goods as final goods for the purposes of calculating GDP.

Because GDP is a measure of domestic production, only goods and services produced within a nation's borders are included in its calculation. Similarly, because GDP is measured for a given period, only goods and services produced during the current year (or the portion of the value produced during the current year) are counted as part of the current year's GDP.

Learning Objective 2: Calculate GDP using the value-added, expenditure, or income methods.

There are three methods for measuring GDP: (1) by aggregating the value added by each firm in the production process, (2) by adding up the total amount spent on final goods and services and subtracting the amount spent on imported goods and services, and (3) by adding labor income and capital income. The **value added** by any firm equals the market value of its product or service minus the cost of inputs purchased from other firms. The value added by each firm represents the portion of the value of the final good or service that the firm creates in its stage of the production process. Summing the value added by all firms in the economy yields the total value of final goods and service, or GDP. An advantage of the value-added method is that it eliminates the problem of dividing the value of a final good or service between two periods.

To calculate GDP using the expenditure method, economic statisticians add together consumption expenditures, investment, government purchases, and net exports. **Consumption expenditure (C)** is spending by households on goods and services. Consumption spending can be divided into three subcategories: (1) consumer durables, long-lived consumer goods such as cars and furniture; (2) consumer nondurables, shorter-lived goods like food and clothing; and (3) services, including everything from haircuts to taxi rides to legal, financial, and educational services. **Investment (*I*)** is spending by firms on final goods and services, primarily capital goods, and housing. Investment is also divided into three subcategories: (1) business fixed investment, the purchase of new capital goods such as machinery, factories, and office buildings; (2) residential investment, the construction of new homes and apartment buildings; and (3) inventory investment, the addition of unsold goods to company inventories. **Government purchases (*G*)** are purchases of final goods by federal, state, and local governments. Government purchases do not include transfer payments (payments made by the government in which no current goods or services are received), or interest paid on the government debt. In the foreign sector, **net exports (*NX*)** equal exports minus imports. Exports are domestically produced final goods and services that are sold abroad. Imports are purchases by domestic buyers of goods and services that were produced abroad. Using symbols for each of the components, the algebraic equation for calculating GDP (*Y*) is written: $Y = C + I + G + NX$.

Hint: When calculating GDP using the expenditure method, be careful to not include in the calculation an expenditure component and one or more of the subcategories. For example, if a dollar value is give for consumption expenditures and for consumer durables, only include the value of the consumption expenditures in your calculation. On the other hand, if no dollar value is given for consumption expenditures, then add together the value of consumer durables, consumer nondurables, and services to calculate the consumption expenditures component of GDP.

The third method of calculating GDP is to sum total labor and capital incomes. Labor income, before taxes includes wages, salaries, and the income of the self-employed. It represents about 75% of GDP. Capital income is made up of payments to the owners of physical capital (factories, machines, and office buildings) and intangible capital (such as copyrights and patents), and it represents about 25% of GDP. The components of capital income include such items as pretax profits earned by business owners, the rents paid to owners of land or buildings, interest received by bondholders, and the royalties received by holders of copyrights or patents.

Learning Objective 3: Define nominal GDP and real GDP.

As a measure of the total production of an economy during a given period, GDP is useful in comparisons of economic activity in different places, but cannot be used to make comparisons over time. To make comparisons of production in an economy over time, GDP must be adjusted for inflation. To adjust for inflation economists differentiate between nominal GDP and real GDP. **Nominal GDP** measures the current dollar value of production, in which the quantities of final goods and services produced are valued at current-year prices. **Real GDP** measures the actual physical volume of production, in which the quantities of final goods and services produced are valued at the prices in a base year.

> **Hint:** Nominal GDP for different years is essentially calculated in two
> different units of measures (e.g., 2002 prices for 2002 GDP and 2003
> prices for 2003 GDP). Because they are two different units of measure
> they are not comparable. Deriving conclusions about the state of the
> economy by comparing nominal GDP for two different periods is the
> equivalent of weighing yourself on two different scales to determine
> whether you had lost or gained weight.

Learning Objective 4: Explain the relationship between GDP and economic well-being.
While economists and policymakers often assume that a higher GDP is better, real GDP is not
the same as economic well-being. With the major exception of government-produced goods and
services, real GDP captures only those goods and services that are priced and sold in markets.
There are many factors that contribute to people's economic well-being that are not priced and
sold in markets. Thus, at best, it is an imperfect measure of economic well-being. Some
important factors that are excluded from real GDP are leisure time; environmental quality;
resource depletion; nonmarket activities such as volunteer services, home-grown foods,
homemaker services, and underground economic activities from informal babysitting to
organized crime; "quality of life" issues such as crime, traffic congestion, civic organization,
open space; and income inequality. Nevertheless, real GDP per person does tend to be positively
associated with many things people value, including a high material standard of living, better
health and life expectancies, and better education.

> **Note:** In evaluating the effects of a proposed economic policy,
> considering only the likely effects on GDP is not sufficient. The correct
> way is to apply the cost-benefit principle.

**Learning Objective 5: Explain how the Bureau of Labor Statistics calculates
unemployment.**
A second macroeconomic measure that receives a great deal of attention from economists and
policymakers, as well as the general public, is the rate of unemployment. In the United States,
the Bureau of Labor Statistics (BLS) conducts a monthly survey of approximately 60,000
households in order to calculate the official unemployment rate. Each person in those households
who is 16 years or older is placed in one of three categories: employed, unemployed, or out of
the labor force. A person is employed if he or she worked full time or part time during the week
preceding the survey, or is on vacation or sick leave from a regular job. A person is unemployed
if he or she did not work during the week preceding the survey, but made some effort to find
work during the previous four weeks. All other persons are considered out of the labor force. In
assessing the impact of unemployment on jobless people, economists estimate how long
individual workers have been without work. The BLS asks respondents how long they have been
continuously unemployed to determine the **unemployment spell**. The length of an
unemployment spell is called its **duration**. The duration of unemployment rises during
recessions and falls during expansions.

Learning Objective 6: Calculate the unemployment rate and participation rate.
To calculate the unemployment rate, the BLS first adds the total number of employed and unemployed people in the economy to determine the size of the **labor force**. The **unemployment rate** is then calculated as the number of unemployed people divided by the labor force and expressed as a percentage. Another useful statistic calculated by the BLS is the **participation rate**, or the percentage of the working-age population that is in the labor force.

Learning Objective 7: Discuss the costs of unemployment.
Unemployment imposes economic, psychological, and social costs on a nation. The main economic cost, borne by both the unemployed individuals and society, is the output that is lost because the work force is not fully utilized. The psychological costs of unemployment are felt primarily by the unemployed workers and their families, and include a loss of self-esteem, feelings of loss of control over one's life, depression, and suicidal behavior. The social costs, borne by both the unemployed individuals and society, include increases in crime, domestic violence, and drug abuse.

Learning Objective 8: Discuss the criticisms of the unemployment rate.
There are some criticisms of the techniques used by the BLS to measure the rate of unemployment. One criticism is that the official unemployment rate understates the true extent of unemployment because of so-called discouraged workers and involuntary part-time workers. **Discouraged workers** are people who say they would like to have a job, but have not made an effort to find one in the previous four weeks. Some observers have suggested that treating discouraged workers as unemployed would provide a more accurate picture of the labor market. **Involuntary part-time workers** are people who say they would like to work full time but are able to find only part-time work.

III. Self-Test

<u>Key Terms</u>
Match the term in the right-hand column with the appropriate definitions in the left-hand column by placing the letter of the term in the blank in front of its definition. (Answers are given at the end of the chapter.)

1. ____Purchases by federal, state, and local governments of final goods and services

a. capital good

2. ____ The percentage of the working-age population in the labor force

b. consumption expenditure

3. ____ Exports minus imports

c. discouraged workers

4. ____ A measure of GDP in which the quantities produced are valued at the prices in a base year rather than at current prices

d. duration (of an unemployment spell)

5. ____ The length of an unemployment spell

e. final goods and services

6. ____ Goods or services consumed by the ultimate user

f. government purchases

7. ____ The total number of employed and unemployed people in the economy

g. gross domestic product (GDP)

8. ____ The market value of any firm's product or service minus the

h. intermediate goods

cost of inputs purchased from other firms   and services
9. ____ People who say they would like to have a job but have not   i. investment
made an effort to find one in the previous 4 weeks
10.____ A measure of GDP in which the quantities produced are   j. labor force
valued at current-year prices
11.____ Spending by firms on final goods and services, primarily   k. net exports
capital goods and housing
12.____ A period during which an individual is continuously   l. nominal GDP
unemployed
13.____ Spending by households on goods and services, such as food, m. participation rate
clothing, and entertainment
14.____ A long-lived good, which is itself produced and used to   n. real GDP
produce other goods and services
15.____ The market value of the final goods and services produced in o. unemployment rate
a country during a given period
16.____ The number of unemployed people divided by the labor force p. unemployment spell
17.____ Goods or services used up in the production of final goods q. value added
and services and therefore not counted as part of GDP

Multiple-Choice Questions
Circle the letter that corresponds to the best answer. (Answers are given at the end of the chapter.)

1. Which of the following would be included in the calculation of GDP for 1996?
    A. the price of a home built in 1991 and sold in 1996
    B. the price of 100 shares of Exxon stock purchased in 1996
    C. the price of a classic 1960 Thunderbird purchased in 1996
    D. the price of a new punch press built and purchased in 1996 to replace a worn out machine
    E. the price of a used bicycle purchased at a garage sale in 1996

2. Which of the following is an intermediate good and, therefore, would be excluded from the calculation of GDP?
    A. a new set of tires sold to a car owner
    B. a new set of tires purchased by Ford to install on a new Explorer
    C. 100 shares of stock in Microsoft
    D. a new home
    E. a preowned automobile

3. The value-added method eliminates the problem of
    A. differentiating between final and intermediate goods and services.
    B. inflation when comparing GDP over time.
    C. determining whether capital is a final good or intermediate good.
    D. dividing the value of a final good or service between two periods.
    E. aggregation.

4. Consumption expenditure is subdivided into three categories, including
   A. consumer durables, consumer nondurables, and new homes.
   B. consumer services, consumer durables, and new homes.
   C. consumer durables, consumer nondurables, and services.
   D. exports, imports, and services.
   E. consumer durables, consumer nondurables, and net exports.

5. Which of the following is included when using the expenditure method to measure GDP?
   A. corporate profits
   B. gross private domestic investment
   C. capital income
   D. net interest on the government debt
   E. labor income

6. Which of the following is included when using the labor and capital income method to measure GDP?
   A. government purchases of goods and services
   B. net exports of goods and services
   C. household consumption expenditures
   D. gross private domestic investment
   E. business profits

7. If the value of imports is greater than the value of exports, then
   A. net exports are negative.
   B. net exports are positive.
   C. net exports are zero.
   D. net exports are not, under such circumstances, included in the calculation of GDP.
   E. net exports cannot be determined from the information provided.

8. To calculate nominal GDP, the quantities of goods and services are valued at prices in the
   _____ year, but to calculate real GDP they are valued at _____-year prices.
   A. current; base
   B. base; current
   C. current; current
   D. base; base
   E. current; last

9. Real GDP is GDP adjusted for
   A. changes in the quality of goods and services.
   B. value added during a previous year.
   C. inflation.
   D. imports.
   E. changes in the cost of intermediate goods and services.

10. One shortcoming of GDP as an indicator of economic well-being is that it fails to measure the
    A. growth in productivity.

    B. increase in the quantity of goods.

    C. nonmarket production.

    D. change in the price level.

    E. increase in the number of imported goods.

11. GDP would be a better measure of economic well-being if it included
    A. the costs of education.
    B. the total value of intermediate goods.
    C. the market value of final goods.
    D. the sales of corporate stock.
    E. leisure.

12. Despite some problems with equating GDP with economic well-being, real GDP per person does imply greater economic well-being because it tends to be positively associated with
    A. crime, pollution, and economic inequality.
    B. better education, health, and life expectancy.
    C. poverty, depletion of nonrenewable resources, and congestion.
    D. unemployment, availability of goods and services, and better education.
    E. the total quantity of goods and services available.

13. The official unemployment rate is calculated as
    A. the number of working-age people 16 years of age or older who are employed divided by the number of people in the labor force.
    B. all people 18 years of age or older who are employed, plus all those unemployed who are actively seeking work.
    C. the percentage of the working-age population 16 years of age or older who are not working but are actively seeking work.
    D. the number of people 16 years of age or older who are not employed and are actively seeking work divided by the number of people in the labor force.
    E. all people 16 years of age or older who are employed, plus all those unemployed who are actively seeking work, divided by the number of people in the labor force.

14. In the monthly survey conducted by the Bureau of Labor Statistics, a person who was not working during the previous week and was not actively seeking work during the previous four weeks is classified as
    A. employed.
    B. unemployed.
    C. underemployed.
    D. part-time employed.
    E. not a member of the labor force.

15. From an economic perspective, the main cost of unemployment is
    A. increased crime, domestic violence, alcoholism, and drug abuse.
    B. a loss of output and income because the labor force is not fully employed.
    C. increased stress, loss of self-esteem, and deterioration in the workers skills from lack of use.
    D. workers' loss of income and control over their lives.

E. the increase in the cost of social programs to combat increased crime, alcoholism, drug abuse, and other social problems.

16. The cost of unemployment that is almost exclusively borne by workers and their families is the _____ cost.
   A. economic
   B. social
   C. psychological
   D. historical
   E. total

17. An unemployment spell begins when a worker
   A. losses his/her job and ends when he/she finds a new job.
   B. losses his/her job and ends when he/she finds a new job or leaves the labor force.
   C. starts to actively look for employment and ends when he/she finds a new job.
   D. is not working and starts to actively look for employment and ends when he/she finds a new job or leaves the labor force.
   E. becomes discouraged and stops seeking employment and ends when he/she begins to actively look for employment.

18. The duration of unemployment
   A. rises during recessions.
   B. falls during recessions.
   C. is a period during which an individual is continuously unemployed.
   D. is shorter for the chronically unemployed than it is for the long-term unemployed.
   E. is of less importance to macroeconomics than the costs of unemployment.

19. The accuracy of the official unemployment rate is criticized because
   A. unemployed homemakers and students who are not actively seeking employment are not included in the number of unemployed people.
   B. people who would like to work but have given up trying to find work are not included in the number of unemployed people.
   C. it fails to indicate how many people work at more than one job.
   D. people less than 16 years of age and over 70 years of age are excluded from the data.
   E. the BLS survey does not include all the households in the United States.

20. In recent years, the Bureau of Labor Statistics has released special unemployment rates that include estimates of the number of discouraged and part-time workers and that indicate that the number of
   A. discouraged workers is insignificant, but the number of part-time workers is significant.
   B. part-time workers is insignificant, but the number of discouraged workers is significant.
   C. part-time workers and discouraged workers is insignificant.
   D. discouraged workers and part-time workers is fairly significant.
   E. discourage workers and part-time workers is decreasing.

Short Answer Problems
(Answers and solutions are given at the end of the chapter.)

1. The Expenditure Approach to GDP
This problem will give you practice calculating GDP using the expenditure method. Use the data in following table to answer the questions below.

Expenditure Components	3rd Quarter, 2002 ($ Bil.)
Business fixed investment	1,109.8
Durable Goods	897.8
Exports	1,038.6
Federal government purchases	697.7
Imports	1,471.5
Inventory investment	17.6
Nondurable goods	2,116.9
Residential investment	469.2
Services	4,346.0
State and local government purchases	1,283.3

Source: U.S. Department of Commerce, Bureau of Economic Analysis. BEA News Release (Gross Domestic Product: Third Quarter 2002 Final – Table)

A. Total consumption spending in the U.S. economy during the third quarter of 2002 equaled
   $_____ billion.
B. Total investment spending in the U.S. economy during the third quarter of 2002 equaled
   $_____ billion.
C. Net export spending in the U.S. economy during the third quarter of 2002 equaled
   $_____ billion.
D. Total government purchases in the U.S. economy during the third quarter of 2002 equaled
   $_____ billion.
E. The expenditure method of calculating indicates that gross domestic product for the U.S.
   economy during the third quarter of 2002 equaled $_____ billion.

2. The Income Approach to GDP
This problem will give you practice calculating GDP using the labor and capital income method. Use the data in following table to answer the questions below.

Income Components	3rd Quarter, 2002 ($ Bil.)
Compensation of employees	6,026.6
Corporate profits	771.0
Net interest	687.6
Proprietor's income	758.7
Rental income	144.1

Source: U.S. Department of Commerce, Bureau of Economic Analysis. <u>BEA News Release</u> (Gross Domestic Product: Third Quarter 2002 Final – Table 8)

A. Total incomes received by the owners of capital during the third quarter of 2002 equaled $_____ billion.

B. Total incomes received by labor during the third quarter of 2002 equaled $_____ billion.

C. The income method of calculating indicates that gross domestic product for the U.S. economy during the third quarter of 2002 equaled $_____ billion.

3. Nominal and Real GDP

This problem will give you practice calculating GDP using the value-added method and adjusting nominal GDP to calculate real GDP.

A. Mr. Jones harvested logs (with no inputs from other companies) from his property in Northern California that he sold to a Nevada Mill for $1,500. The Nevada Mill cut and planed the logs into lumber and sold it for $4,000 to the Mesa Company, to be used to build tables. The Mesa Company used the lumber in producing 100 tables that they sold to customers for $70 each. Complete the table below to calculate the value added by each firm.

Company	Revenues	Cost of purchased inputs	Value added
Mr. Jones			
Nevada Mill			
Mesa Company			

B. The total value added in the production of the tables equals $_____ . This is equal to the _____ of the 100 tables.

C. If Mr. Jones had harvested the logs in October of 2000 but did not sell them to the Nevada Mill until January 2001, which then sold the lumber to Mesa Company that produced the tables in June 2001, the contribution to GDP in 2000 would equal $_____ and in 2001 would equal $_____ .

D. The nation of Mandar specializes in the production of vehicles. The table below provides data on the prices and quantities of the vehicles produced in 2001 and in 2003. Assume that 2001 is the base year. In 2001, nominal GDP equals $_____ and in 2003 it equals $_____ . In 2001, real GDP equals $_____ and in 2003 it equals $_____ .

	Bicycles		Automobiles		Trucks	
Year	Quantity	Price	Quantity	Price	Quantity	Price
2001	1,000	$50	100	$10,000	400	$15,000
2003	1,500	$60	50	$12,500	500	$15,000

4. Measures of Employment

This problem will give you practice in calculating employment measures. Use the data in following table to answer the questions below.

Year	Employed	Unemployed	Not in Labor Force	Working Age Population	Labor Force	Unemployment rate (%)	Participation rate (%)
1997	129,558	6,739	66,837				
1998	131,463	6,210	67,547				
1999	133,488	5,880	68,385				
2000	135,208	5,655	68,836				
2001	135,073	6,742	70,050				

Source: *Economic Report of the President,* February 2002, Table b-35

A. Calculate the working age population for 1997 through 2002 to complete column 5 of the table.
B. Calculate the size of the labor force for 1997 through 2002 to complete column 6 of the table.
C. Calculate the official unemployment rate for 1997 through 2002 to complete column 7 of the table. (Round your answers to the nearest tenth of a percent.)
D. Calculate the participation rate for 1997 through 2002 to complete column 8 of the table. (Round your answers to the nearest tenth of a percent.)

IV. Economic Naturalist Application

Economic Naturalist 5.5 states that the opportunity cost of sending children to school is higher in low-income agrarian societies the than in high-income nonagricultural countries. The following data from the United Nations Department of Economic and Social Indicators give the per capita income in 2000 (in the equivalent of U.S. dollars) and expected number of years of formal schooling: Canada $22,778, 14.8; Denmark $30,141, 15.6; Ethiopia $102, 4.3; Greece $10,680, 14.3; Latvia $2,952, 11.2. Is the statement supported by the data? Explain your answer.
Answer

V. Go to the Web: Graphing Exercises Using Interactive Graphs

Which is Better, Real GDP or Nominal GDP?

Which is the better measure of economic activity, real GDP or nominal GDP? Why?
Answer:

To learn more about the use of economic theory to analyze this issue (and other macroeconomic issues), please go to the Electronic Learning Session in the Student Center at the Frank/Bernanke web site: http://www.mhhe.com/economics/frankbernanke2.

VI. Self-Test Solutions

Key Terms
1. f
2. m
3. k
4. n
5. d
6. e
7. j
8. q
9. c
10. l
11. i
12. o
13. b
14. a
15. g
16. p
17. h

Multiple-Choice Questions
1. D The punch press is newly produced capital.
2. B
3. D
4. C
5. B
6. E Profit is a component of capital income.
7. A
8. A
9. C
10. C
11. E
12. B
13. D
14. B
15. B
16. C
17. D An unemployment spell begins when a person becomes unemployed and ends when he or she either becomes employed or leaves the labor force.
18. A
19. B

20. C

Short Answer Problems
1.
A. $897.8 + $2,116.9 + $4,346.0 = $7,360.7 billion
B. $1,109.8 + $469.9 + 17.6 = $1,597.3 billion
C. $ 1,038.6– $1,471.5 = $-432.9 billion
D. $697.7+ $1,283.3= $1,981.0 billion
E. $7,360.7 + 1,597.3 + 1,981.0 + $-432.9) = $10,506.1 billion

2.
A. $771.0+ 687.6+ 144.1= $1,602.7 billion
B. $6,026.6+ 758.7 = $6,785.3 billion
C. $1,602.7 + 6,785.3 = $ 8,388.0 billion [The difference between the answer in 2C and 1E is attributable to some technical adjustments that are not covered in the textbook.]

3.A.

Company	Revenues	Cost of purchased inputs	Value added
Mr. Jones	$1,500	$0	1,500
Nevada Mill	$4,000	$1,500	$2,500
Mesa Company	$7,000	$4,000	$3,000

B. $7,000; total market value
C. $1,500; $2,500 + $3,000 = $5,500
D. 1,000 x $50 + 100 x $10,000 + 400 x $15,000 = $7,050,000; 1,500 x $60 + 50 x $12,500 + 500 x $15,000 = $8,215,000; 1,000 x $50 + 100 x $10,000 + 400 x $15,000 = $7,050,000; 1,500 x $50 + 50 x $10,000 + 500 x $15,000 = $8,075,000

4.
A. Working age population = number of persons employed + number of persons unemployed + number of persons not in the labor force (1997: 129,558 + 6,739 + 66,837 = 203,134)
B. Labor force = number of persons employed + number of persons unemployed (for example, 1997: 129,558 + 6,739 = 136,297)
C. Unemployment rate = (number of persons unemployed divided by number of persons not in the labor force) times 100 (for example, 1997: (6,739 / 136,297) x 100 = 4.9%)
D. Participation rate = (number of persons in the labor force divided by Working age population) times 100 (for example, 1997: (136,297/ 203,134) x 100 = 67.1%)

Year	Employed	Unemployed	Not in Labor Force	Working Age Population	Labor Force	Unemployment rate (%)	Participation rate (%)
1997	129,558	6,739	66,837	203,134	136,297	4.9	67.1
1998	131,463	6,210	67,547	205,220	137,673	4.5	67.1
1999	133,488	5,880	68,385	207,753	139,368	4.2	67.1
2000	135,208	5,655	68,836	209,699	140,863	4.0	67.2
2001	135,073	6,742	70,050	211,865	141,815	4.8	66.9

Chapter 6
Measuring the Price Level and Inflation

I. Pretest: What Do You Really Know?
Circle the letter that corresponds to the best answer. (Answers appear immediately after the final question).

1. A measure of the average price of a given class of goods or services relative to the price of the same goods and services in a base year is called a
    A. real price.
    B. real quantity.
    C. rate of inflation.
    D. price level.
    E. price index.

2. The consumer price index for Planet Econ consists of only two items: books and hamburgers. In 1999, the base year, the typical consumer purchased 5 books for $20 each and 30 hamburgers for $1 each. In 2000, the typical consumer purchased 8 books for $22 each and 36 hamburgers for $1.50 each. The consumer price index for 2000 on Planet Econ equals
    A. 1.00
    B. 1.08
    C. 1.15
    D. 1.23
    E. 1.77

3. The CPI in year one equaled 1.45. The CPI in year two equaled 1.53. The rate of inflation between years one and two was _____ percent.
    A. 4.0
    B. 4.5
    C. 5.3
    D. 5.5
    E. 8.0

4. The situation when the price of most goods and services are falling over time is called
    A. inflation.
    B. disinflation.
    C. a boom.
    D. deflation.
    E. an expansion.

5. A quantity measured in terms of current dollar value is called a _____ quantity.
    A. nominal
    B. real
    C. deflated
    D. indexed
    E. relative

6. All of the following are real quantities *except* the
    A. number of new cars produced in one year.
    B. tons of steel shipped to South America.
    C. millions of computer chips shipped to computer makers.
    D. billions of dollars invested in stocks.
    E. truckloads of oranges used to manufacture juice.

7. A college graduate in 1972 found a job paying $10,000. The CPI was 0.418 in 1972. A
    college graduate in 2000 found a job paying $30,000. The CPI was 1.68 in 2000. The 1972
    graduate's job paid ____ in nominal terms and _____ in real terms than the 2000 graduate's
    job.
    A. more; less
    B. more; more
    C. less; the same
    D. less, more
    E. less, less

8. The real wage is the wage
    A. measured in current dollars.
    B. required to maintain a minimum standard of living.
    C. employers are required to pay workers.
    D. measured in terms of purchasing power.
    E. the federal government sets as the minimum wage.

9. The CPI equals 1.00 in year one and 1.20 in year two. If the nominal wage is $15 in year one
    and a contract calls for the wage to be indexed to the CPI , what will be the nominal wage in
    year two?
    A. $12.50
    B. $15.00
    C. $15.20
    D. $17.25
    E. $18.00

10. If the Boskin Commission's conclusion that the CPI _____ the "true" inflation rate is correct, then indexing Social Security benefits to the CPI is ____ the federal government billions of dollars.
    A. understates; costing
    B. understates; saving
    C. measures; saving
    D. overstates; costing
    E. overstates; saving

Solutions and Feedback to Pretest

For each question you incorrectly answered, we strongly recommend taking the time to review the appropriate material before continuing. In the table below, the relevant textbook pages are listed for each question as well as the pertinent Learning Objective from the following Key Point Review.

Correct Answer	Textbook Page Numbers	Learning Objective
1. E	p. 139	1
2. E	p. 141	1
3. D	pp. 142-43	2
4. D	p. 143	1
5. A	p. 144	3
6. D	p. 144	3
7. D	p. 144-45	3
8. D	p. 145	3
9. E	p. 146	3
10. D	pp. 146-49	5

II. Key Point Review

This chapter continues the study of the construction and interpretation of macroeconomic data. The topics discussed are measuring prices and inflation, adjusting dollar amounts to eliminate the effects of inflation, using a price index to maintain the constant real value of a variable, the costs of inflation, and the relationship between inflation and interest rates.

Learning Objective 1: Define price index, inflation and deflation, and explain how the Bureaus of Labor Statistics estimates the Consumer Price Index.

The basic tool economists use to measure the price level and inflation in the U.S. economy is the consumer price index, or CPI. The CPI is an **index**, a measure of the average price of a given class of goods or services relative to the price of the same goods and services in a base year. The **consumer price index** measures the cost, for any period, of a standard basket of goods and services relative to the cost of the same basket of goods and services in a fixed year, called the base year. The Bureaus of Labor Statistics (BLS) determines the goods and services to include in the standard basket through the Consumer Expenditure Survey. Then each month BLS employees survey thousands of stores to determine the current prices of the goods and services. The formula for calculating the CPI is "cost of the base-year basket of goods and services in the current year" divided by the "cost of the base-year basket of goods and services in the base year."

> **Note**: When calculating consumer price indices for a multiyear period, the denominator will be the **same** value (the cost of the base-year basket of goods and services) for each calculation.

Inflation measures how fast the average price level is rising over time. The rate of **inflation** is defined as the annual percentage rate of change in the price level, as measured, for example, by the CPI. **Deflation** is a situation in which the prices of most goods and services are falling over time, so that the rate of inflation is negative.

Learning Objective 2: Use the CPI to calculate the rate of inflation and explain why using the CPI to calculate the inflation rate may overstate the true inflation.
The inflation rate is calculated for a specific time period (e.g., a year) by subtracting the price index of an earlier time period from the price index of a more recent time period (e.g., CPI in 2002 minus the CPI in 2001) and dividing the change in the price index by the price index in the earlier time period (e.g., CPI in 2001).

> **Hint**: When calculating the inflation rate for a multiyear period, the denominator will **NOT** be the same value for each calculation. The inflation rate is calculated by dividing the change in the price index by the price index at the end of the previous year. Students sometimes confuse the calculation of inflation rates with calculating the CPI and mistakenly use the base year price index to calculate a series of inflation rates.

Using the CPI to measure inflation has not been without controversy. Because the CPI has been used to index Social Security benefits, the U.S. government commissioned a report on the subject. The Boskin Commission concluded that the official CPI inflation overstates the true inflation rate by as much as one to two percent per year. The CPI may overstate inflation because of the quality adjustment bias and the substitution bias. Quality adjustment bias refers to the inability of government statisticians to adequately adjust the data for changes in product quality. The substitution bias arises from the fact that the CPI is calculated from a fixed basket of goods and services and, thus, does not allow for the possibility that consumers can switch from products whose prices are rising to those whose prices are stable or falling.

Learning Objective 3: Define indexing and deflating.

The CPI not only allows us to measure changes in the cost of living, but can also be used to adjust economic data to eliminate the effects of inflation, a process called **deflating**. To adjust a **nominal quantity**, a quantity that is measured at its current dollar value, we divide the nominal quantity by a price index for the period. The adjusted value is called a **real quantity**, that is, a quantity measured in physical terms. Such real quantities are also sometimes referred to as inflation-adjusted quantities. For example, nominal wages for two different periods can be adjusted using the CPI to determine the change in real wages over time. The **real wage** is the wage paid to workers measured in terms of real purchasing power. To calculate the real wage we divide the nominal (dollar) wage by the CPI for that period. The CPI can also be used to convert real quantities to nominal quantities. The practice of increasing a nominal quantity according to changes in a price index in order to prevent inflation from eroding purchasing power is called **indexing**. For example, some labor contracts provide for indexing of wages, using the CPI, in later years of a contract period.

Note: Deflating and indexing are essentially opposite means of compensating for inflation. Deflating removes the monetary value of past inflation, while indexing adds in the monetary value of potential future inflation.

Learning Objective 4: Distinguish between price level and relative price.

The **price level** is a measure of the overall level of prices in the economy at a particular point in time, as measured by a price index (e.g., the CPI). The **relative price** of a specific good or service is its price in comparison to the prices of other goods and services. Inflation is an increase in the overall price level, not an increase in the relative price of a good or service. Understanding the difference between the price level and the relative price of a good or service is necessary in order to explain the costs of inflation.

Note: Changes in the price level are generally believed to impose costs on society with little or no benefits, while changes in relative prices are generally believed to be beneficial to the economy with little or no costs.

Learning Objective 5: Explain the five costs of inflation.

When an economy suffers from inflation, the cost of holding cash increases and causes consumers and businesses to make more frequent trips to the bank, and to purchase cash-management systems. Banks will, therefore, hire more employees to handle the increased transactions. These costs of economizing on cash have been called shoe-leather costs. Inflation also creates "noise" in the price system that obscures the information transmitted by prices, reduces the efficiency of the market system, and imposes costs on the economy. Similarly, inflation produces unintended changes in the tax people pay and distorts the incentives in the tax system that may encourage people to work, save, and invest. Another concern about inflation is that, if it is unanticipated, it arbitrarily redistributes wealth from one group to another (e.g., between lenders and borrowers, and workers and employers). As a result, a high inflation economy encourages people to use resources in trying to anticipate inflation to protect themselves against losses of wealth. The fifth cost of inflation is its tendency to interfere with the long-run planning of households and firms. While any inflation imposes some costs on the economy, **hyperinflation**, a situation in which the inflation rate is extremely high, greatly magnifies the costs.

Learning Objective 5: Discuss the relationship between the inflation rate and interest rates.
An important aspect of inflation is its effect on interest rates. To understand the relationship between inflation and interest rates, economists differentiate between the **nominal interest rate** and the **real interest rate.** The nominal interest rate (also called the market interest rate) is the annual percentage increase in the nominal value of a financial asset. The real interest rate is the annual percentage increase in the purchasing power of a financial asset, and is equal to the nominal interest rate minus the inflation rate. To obtain a given real interest rate, lenders must charge a higher nominal interest rate as the inflation rate rises. This tendency for nominal interest rates to rise when the inflation rate increases is called the **Fischer effect.**

Hint: In order to correctly understand the relationship between the inflation rate and interest rates, it is important to recognize that the inflation rate is the independent variable (the causal factor) and interest rates are the dependent variable (the effect). Thus, it is **not** correct to say that an increase in interest rates causes higher inflation rates.

I. Self-Test

Key Terms
Match the term in the right-hand column with the appropriate definitions in the left-hand column by placing the letter of the term in the blank in front of its definition. (Answers are given at the end of the chapter.)

1. _____ The wage paid to workers measured in terms of real purchasing power.

2. _____ The tendency for nominal interest rates to be high when inflation is high and low when inflation is low.

3. _____ A measure of the overall level of prices at a particular point in time as measured by a price index such as the CPI.

4. _____ A situation in which the prices of most goods and services are falling over time so that inflation is negative.

5. _____ The practice of increasing a nominal quantity each period by an amount equal to the percentage increase in a specified price index.

6. _____ A quantity that is measured in physical terms – for example, in terms of quantities of goods and services.

7. _____ The annual percentage increase in the nominal value of a financial asset.

8. _____ A situation in which the inflation rate is extremely high.

a. consumer price index (CPI)

b. deflating (a nominal quantity)

c. deflation

d. Fisher effect

e. hyperinflation

f. indexing

g. nominal interest rate

h. nominal quantity

basket of goods and services relative to the cost of the same basket of goods and services in a fixed year, called the base year.

10.____ The annual percentage rate of change in the price level, as measured, for example by the CPI.

j. price level

11.____ A quantity that is measured in terms of its current dollar value.

k. rate of inflation

12.____The process of dividing a nominal quantity by a price index (such as the CPI) to express the quantity in real terms.

l. real interest rate

13.____ The annual percentage increase in the purchasing power of a financial asset.

m. real quantity

14.____ A measure of the average price of a given class of goods and services relative to the price of the same goods and services in a base year.

n. real wage

15.____ The price of a specific good or service in comparison to the prices of other goods and services.

o. relative price

Multiple-Choice Questions
Circle the letter that corresponds to the best answer. (Answers are given at the end of the chapter.)

1. Inflation exists when
   A) and only when the prices of all goods and services are rising.
   B) the purchasing power of money is increasing.
   C) the average price level is rising, although some prices may be falling.
   D) the prices of basic necessities are increasing.
   E) wages and the price of oil are rising.

2. If the CPI is 125 at the end of 2000 and equals 150 at the end of 2001, then the inflation rate for 2001 would equal
   A) 15 percent.
   B) 20 percent.
   C) 25 percent
   D) 125 percent.
   E) 150 percent.

3. If the Consumer Price Index (CPI) overstates the true rate of inflation, the use of the CPI to adjust nominal incomes results in
   A) understating gains in real incomes.
   B) overstating gains in real incomes.
   C) an accurate statement of gains in real incomes.
   D) nominal values equaling real values.
   E) an arbitrary redistribution of income.

4. Which of the following statements is true about the relationship between a nominal quantity and a real quantity?
    A) A real quantity indicates the amount of money received, while a nominal quantity indicates the real quantity's purchasing power.
    B) A nominal quantity is measured in current dollar values, but a real quantity is measured in terms of physical quantity.
    C) A nominal quantity is adjusted for inflation; a real quantity is not.
    D) A real quantity minus a nominal quantity equals purchasing power.
    E) There is no difference; nominal quantity and real quantity are two different terms for the purchasing power of money.

5. If the Consumer Price Index decreases
    A) the purchasing power of money decreases.
    B) a dollar will buy fewer goods and services.
    C) real income equals nominal income.
    D) there is inflation.
    E) there is deflation.

6. If you borrow money at what you believe is an appropriate interest rate for the level of expected inflation, but the actual inflation rate turns out to be much higher than you had expected. the
    A) loan will be paid back with dollars that have much higher purchasing power than you had expected.
    B) loan will be paid back with dollars that have the same purchasing power as the dollars you borrowed.
    C) borrower's and lender's wealth will have been destroyed by the higher inflation.
    D) borrower will gain from an unintended redistribution of wealth.
    E) borrower will unintentionally redistribute wealth to the lender.

7. If, in a given period, the rate of inflation turns out to be lower than lenders and borrowers anticipated, the effect is that
    A) the real payments by the borrowers will be lower than expected.
    B) the nominal income of lenders will be higher than expected, but their real income will be lower than expected.
    C) the nominal income of the lenders will be as expected, but their real income will be higher than expected.
    D) both the nominal and real income of lenders will be higher than expected.
    E) the real income of lenders will be higher than expected, but their nominal income will be lower than expected.

8. The Consumer Price Index is a measure of the change in prices of
    A) a standard basket of all goods and services.
    B) a standard basket of goods determined by the Consumer Expenditure Survey.
    C) a standard basket of agricultural goods determined by the Consumer Expenditure Survey.
    D) a standard basket of selected items in wholesale markets.
    E) a standard basket of machinery, tools, and new plant.

9. "Shoe leather" costs of inflation refer to the
   A) difficulty of interpreting the price signals in an inflationary environment.
   B) unintended changes in taxes caused by inflation.
   C) arbitrary redistribution of wealth from one group to another.
   D) costs of economizing on holding cash.
   E) interference of inflation on the long-run planning of households and businesses.

10. The CPI for a given year measures the cost of living in that year relative to
    A) what it was in the base year.
    B) what it was in the previous year.
    C) the cost of the basic goods and services need to sustain a typical household.
    D) the amount spent on goods and services by the randomly selected families in the Consumer Expenditure Survey.
    E) the cost of the basic goods and services in the base year.

11. When comparing the money wages of today's workers to money wages workers earned 10 years ago, it is necessary to adjust the nominal wages by
    A) indexing the money wages in each period to today's price index.
    B) deflating the money wages in each period with today's price index.
    C) indexing the money wages in each period with the price indexes of the respective periods.
    D) deflating the money wages in each period with the price indexes of the respective periods.
    E) deflating the money wages in each period with the price index of the past period.

12. The Boskin Commission reported that the official inflation rate, based on the CPI, might overstate true inflation. It identified two reasons, including the
    A) quality adjustment bias and the indexing bias
    B) quality adjustment bias and the substitution bias.
    C) substitution bias and the indexing bias.
    D) quality adjustment bias and the deflation bias.
    E) indexing bias and deflation bias.

13. During the last half of 1999 and first quarter of 2000, the members of the Organization of Petroleum Exporting Countries (OPEC) negotiated reductions in the global production of oil. As a result, the price of heating oil and gasoline increased dramatically in the United States during that period. This led some analysts to predict an increase in the inflation rate in the United States. Drawing such a conclusion results from confusing
    A) inflation with indexing.
    B) inflation with deflation.
    C) a change in the relative price of a good with a change in the price level.
    D) a change in the relative price level with a change in the absolute price level.
    E) indexing with deflating.

14. Inflation creates static or "noise" in the price system, making it difficult for
    A) businesses and households to make long-term plans.
    B) lenders and borrowers to determine an appropriate level of nominal interest rate on loans.

C) employers and workers to determine the appropriate level of money wages to be paid.

D) businesses to interpret the information being transmitted by price changes.

E) households and businesses to hold cash.

15. The real interest rate can be written in mathematical terms as
   A) $r = i - \pi$
   B) $r = \pi - i$
   C) $r = i + \pi$
   D) $r = \pi + i$
   E) $r = i / \pi$

16. In the United States during the 1970s, nominal interest rates were
   A) falling and real interest rates were falling.
   B) rising and real interest rates were rising.
   C) falling and real interest rates were rising.
   D) rising and real interest rates were falling.
   E) rising and real interest rates became negative.

17. If the Consumer Price Index is 135 at the end of 2001 and at the end of 2002 it is 142, then during 2002 the economy experienced
   A) deflation
   B) inflation
   C) hyperinflation
   D) indexing
   E) deflating

18. Mr. Long is considering the purchase of a corporate bond with a yield (interest rate) of 6% per year, and he expects the inflation rate will average 4% per year during the period that he would hold the bond. Mr. Long has decided to purchase the bond only if the real rate of return is positive on the investment. If the tax rate on the interest income is
   A) greater than 33.3%, he should buy the bond.
   B) greater than 50%, he should buy the bond.
   C) less than 33.3%, he should buy the bond.
   D) less than 50%, he should buy the bond.
   E) less than 33.3%, he should not buy the bond.

19. Ms. Savior bought 300 shares of stock in the Dot.com Company in 2000 for $1,000. In 2002 she sold the shares for $1,050, earning $50 in capital gains. She must pay a 20% capital gains tax, leaving her with a net gain of $40. During the two years that she held the stock the price level rose by 4%. As a result her real return on the stock was
   A) positive.
   B) negative.
   C) zero.
   D) greater than the nominal yield (interest rate).
   E) equal to the nominal yield (interest rate).

20. According to the Fisher Effect
    A) high interest rates will cause high inflation rates.
    B) high inflation rates will cause high interest rates.
    C) low interest rates will cause high inflation rates.
    D) low interest rates will cause low inflation rates.
    E) low inflation rates will cause high interest rates.

Short Answer Problems
(Answers and solutions are given at the end of the chapter.)

1. Consumer Price Index and Inflation
The data in the following table are taken from the U.S. Consumer Expenditure Survey conducted by the Bureau of Labor Statistics. The "Average Annual Expenditure" refers to the cost of purchasing the standard market basket of goods and services by the typical household in the United States in each year.

Year	Average Annual Expenditure	Consumer Price Index	Inflation rate (%)	After-tax Income	After-tax Real Income
2001	$39,518			$44,587	
2000	38,045			41,532	
1999	36,995			40,652	
1998	35,535			38,358	
1997	34,819			36,584	

A. Using 1998 as the base year, complete column three of the table by calculating the Consumer Price Index for 1997-2001.

B. Complete column 4 of the table by calculating the inflation rates for 1998-2001.

C. In the same survey, the BLS provides the average nominal income after paying taxes of the typical household, shown in column 5 of the table. Using the CPI to adjust the nominal income, complete column 6 of the table by calculating the after-tax real income of the typical household for 1997-2001.

D. In which of the years from 1997-2001was the typical household in the United States economically best off? _____ .

E. In which of the years from 1997-2001was the typical household in the United States economically worst off? _____

2. Costs of Higher Education
Deloitte and Touche, LLP (an accounting firm) estimated the average cost of college during 1994-95 for four-year public and private institutions. The data is shown in the table below.

Categories	Public Colleges	Private Colleges
Tuition and fees	$2,686	$11,709
Books and Supplies	578	585

Room and Board	3,826	4,976
Transportation	592	523
Other	1,308	991
Total Cost	**$8,990**	**$18,784**

A. In the year 2000-01, it has also estimated that the total cost of attending a public college was $14,266 and a private college was $33,277. Using 1994-95 as the base year, calculate the price index for attending public and private colleges. Price index for public college 1994-95 _____ ; price index for private college 1994-95 _____; price index for public college 2000-01_____; price index for public college 2000-01 _____ .

B. What was the percentage increase in the cost of attending a public college between 1994-95 and 2000-01? _____ percent. What was the percentage increase in the cost of attending a private college between 1994-95 and 2000-01? _____ percent.

C. Sam attended a public college in his home state beginning in 1994-95 and graduating in 2000-01. He paid the cost of his college education by working part time and summers as a firefighter. When he entered college his nominal (money) income was $13,000 and the year he graduated his nominal income had risen to $15,500. Because the cost of college includes all his living expenses, the price index for attending a public college represents his cost of living index. Thus, his real income (measured in 1994-95 dollars) in 1994-95 was $_____ and in 2000-01 it was $_____ .

D. Was Sam economically better off during the year he graduated or the year he entered college? Explain your answer. _____

D. Sue attended a private college outside of her home state beginning in 1994-95 and she also graduated in 2000-01. She paid the cost of her college education by working part time and summers as a consultant designing web pages. When she entered college her nominal (money) income was $40,000. Because the cost of college includes all her living expenses, the price index for attending a private college represents her cost of living index. If her real income was to remain constant from 1994-95 through 2000-01, her nominal income in 2000-01 would have had to rise to $_____ .

3. Nominal and Real Interest Rates
Answer the questions below based on the data in the following table. The table shows the inflation rate in the United States, measured by the GDP deflator index, and nominal interest rates, measured by the yield on the 30-year Treasury bond.

Year	Inflation rate	Interest rate
1996	1.88	6.88
1992	2.75	8.14
1988	3.65	8.58
1984	3.77	11.18
1980	9.23	9.29

A. In what year was the real interest rate on the 30-year Treasury bond the highest? _____
B. In what year did the financial investors who bought the 30-year Treasury bonds get the best deal? _____
C. In what year was the real interest rate on the 30-year Treasury bond the lowest, but still positive? _____
D. In what year did the financial investors who bought the 30-year Treasury bonds get the worst deal? _____
E. What was the real interest rate on the 30-year Treasury bond in 1996? _____ %

IV. Economic Naturalist Application

In Economic Naturalist 6.1, the textbook authors discuss the political implications of the minimum wage not being indexed to inflation. The table below shows the historical nominal minimum wage and the CPI from 1960 to 2000. Answer the questions below using the data in the following table to determine the economic implications of the minimum wage not being indexed to inflation.

Year	Nominal Minimum Wage	CPI ('82-84 =100)
1960	$1.00	29.6
1965	$1.25	31.5
1970	$1.60	38.8
1975	$2.10	53.8
1980	$3.10	82.4
1985	$3.35	107.6
1990	$3.80	130.7
1995	$4.25	152.4
2000	$5.15	172.2

In which of the years shown in the table was the real value of the minimum wage highest? In which of the years shown in the table was the real value of the minimum wage lowest? During which two time periods was the real value of the minimum wage rising? During which time period was the real value of the minimum wage rising? In which year, 1960 or 2000, did minimum wage earners have the highest purchasing power?
Answers:

V. Go to the Web: Graphing Exercises Using Interactive Graphs

Changes in Consumer Spending and the CPI

The CPI for a given period measures the cost of living for that period relative to what it was in the base year, for a given market basket of goods and services. What happens when consumers respond to price changes by changing their purchases? How does this affect a family's actual cost of living and the CPI?
Answer:

To review the answer to this question and learn more about the use of economic theory to analyze macroeconomic issues please go to the Electronic Learning Session in the Student Center at the Frank/Bernanke web site: http://www.mhhe.com/economics/frankbernanke2.

V. Self -Test Solutions

Key Terms
1. n
2. d
3. j
4. c
5. f
6. m
7. g
8. e
9. a
10. k
11. h
12. b
13. l
14. i
15. o

Multiple-Choice Questions
1. C
2. B The inflation rate = $(150 - 125)/125 = 25/125 = .20$ or 20%
3. A If the true inflation rate is less than the official measure of inflation, then the real income would be greater than the official data would suggest.
4. B
5. E

6. D The borrower gains from being able to pay back the loan in less valuable dollars.
7. C
8. B
9. D
10. A
11. D
12. B
13. C The changes in the prices of gasoline and heating oil are changes in relative prices, not changes in the price level that would indicate inflation.
14. D
15. A r = real interest rate; i = nominal, or market, interest rate; and π = inflation rate
16. E
17. B
18. C If the tax rate is 33.3% or greater, Mr. Long will pay the equivalent of 2% or more in income taxes, leaving him an after-tax nominal return of 4% or less. Subtracting the 4% expected inflation would result in a zero or negative real return on the investment. Since he decided to only invest if the real return was positive he should only buy the bond if the tax rate is less than 33.3%.
19. C The $40 after-tax return divided by the $1,000 price of the bond equals a nominal rate of return of 4%. Subtracting the inflation rate of 4% would give her a real return of zero.
20. B

Short Answer Problems
1.
A. CPI = (cost of the base-year basket of goods and services in the current year) divided by (cost of the base-year basket of goods and services in the base year) . For example, 2001 CPI = $39,518 / $35,535 = 1.11
B. inflation rate = (CPI in year – CPI in previous year) / CPI in previous year. For example, 2001 inflation rate = (1.11 – 1.07) / 1.07 = 3.73%
C. real income = nominal income / price index. For example, 2001 After tax real income = $44,587/ 1.11= $40,093.10

Year	Average Annual Expenditure	Consumer Price Index	Inflation rate (%)	After-tax Income	After-tax Real Income
2001	$39,518	1.11	3.73	$44,587	$40,093.10
2000	38,045	1.07	2.76	41,532	$38,791.95
1999	36,995	1.04	3.95	40,652	$39,047.68
1998	35,535	1.00	2.01	38,358	$38,358.00
1997	34,819	0.98	XXX	36,584	$37,336.29

D. 2001
E. 1997

2.
A. price index = $8.990/$8,990 = 1.00; $14,266/$8,990 = 1.59; 1.00; 1.77
B. percentage change = ($14,266- $8,990)/ $8,990 =58.7%; 77.2%

C. real income = $13,000 / 1.00 = $13,000; $9,767.63

D. during his first year

E. To determine how much her income would need to rise by, you need to index her income during the first year of school by multiplying it times the price index for private college during year she graduated, (i.e., $40,000 x 1.77 = $70,862.44).

3.

A. 1984

B. 1984

C. 1980

D. 1980

E. 5% (= 6.88 – 1.88)

Chapter 7
Economic Growth, Productivity, and Living Standards

I. Pretest: What Do You Really Know?

Circle the letter that corresponds to the best answer. (Answers appear immediately after the final question).

1. The key indicator of a country's living standard and economic well being is
   A. the unemployment rate.
   B. the inflation rate.
   C. real GDP.
   D. real GDP per person.
   E. average labor productivity.

2. Real GDP per person in Westland is $15,000, while real GDP in Eastland is $20,000, However, Westland's real GDP per person is growing at 2.5 % per year and Eastland's is growing at 1.5% per year. If these growth rates persist indefinitely, then
   A. Westland's real GDP per person will increase until it equals, but does not exceed, Eastland's.
   B. Westland's real GDP per person will eventually be greater than Eastland's.
   C. Eastland's real GDP per person will always be greater than Westland's.
   D. Eastland's real GDP per person will decline until it equals Westland's.
   E. Eastland's real GDP per person will decline, but never be less than Westland's.

3. If real GDP per person equaled $1,000 in 1900 and grew at a 4 percent annual rate, what would real GDP equal 100 years later?
   A. $4,040
   B. $5,100
   C. $8,705
   D. $50,505
   E. $4,780,612

4. The payment of interest not only on the original deposit, but on all previously accumulated interest is called
   A. the real interest rate.
   B. the nominal interest rate.
   C. simple interest.
   D. conflict of interest.
   E. compound interest.

5. If when you are 21 you put $1,000 in a bank deposit promising to pay 8 percent annual compound interest, how much will be in the account 45 years later when you retire at age 66?
   A. $4,600
   B. $13,765
   C. $31,920
   D. $48,600
   E. $86,962

6. Growth of real GDP per person is totally determined by the growth of average
   A. labor productivity and the proportion of the population employed.
   B. labor productivity and the proportion of the population in the labor force.
   C. labor force participation and the share of income going to capital.
   D. labor force participation and the share of the population employed.
   E. number of employed workers and population.

7. In Macroland 400,000 of the 1 million people in the country are employed. Average labor productivity in Macroland is $30,000 per worker. Real GDP per person in Macroland totals
   A. $1,000
   B. $12,000
   C. $15,000
   D. $30,000
   E. $42,000

8. Average labor productivity is determined by
   A. consumption, investment, government spending, and net exports.
   B. the number employed, unemployed, and the labor force participation rate.
   C. the quantity and quality of human capital, physical capital, technology, natural resources, entrepreneurship, and the legal and political environment.
   D. the real interest rate, the nominal interest rate, and the rate of inflation.
   E. the difference between government spending and revenues.

9. Mike and Tom debone chicken breasts for Ted's Chicken Co. Mike is new and can only debone 20 chicken breasts per hour, while Tom's experience allows him to debone 50 chicken breasts per hour. Both Mike and Tom work 40 hours per week. Their average hourly productivity as a team is _____ chicken breasts.
    A. 30
    B. 35
    C. 70
    D. 90
    E. 140

10. Countries with large amounts of capital per worker tend to have _____ levels of real GDP per person and _____ levels of average labor productivity.
    A. high; high
    B. high; low
    C. low; low
    D. low; average
    E. low; high

Solutions and Feedback to Pretest

For each question you incorrectly answered, we strongly recommend taking the time to review the appropriate material before continuing. In the table below, the relevant textbook pages are listed for each question as well as the pertinent Learning Objective from the following Key Point Review.

Correct Answer	Textbook Page Numbers	Learning Objective
1. B	pp. 171 - 72	1
2. B	pp. 172 - 73	2
3. D	pp. 172 - 73	2
4. E	pp. 172 - 73	2
5. C	pp. 172 - 73	2
6. A	p. 174	3
7. B	p. 174	3
8. C	pp. 176 - 84	4
9. B	p. 174	3
10. A	pp. 176 - 84	4

II. Key Point Review

Over the past two centuries a radical transformation has occurred in the living standards of people in the industrialized countries that has resulted from a remarkable rise in the economic growth rates of those nations. This chapter explores the sources of economic growth and rising standards of living in the modern world. Secondary issues discussed include government policies to promote economic growth, the costs of rapid economic growth, and whether there may be limits to economic growth.

Learning Objective 1: Compare rates of growth in real GDP per person among countries during the 19th and 20th centuries.

Despite the recognition that it is an imperfect measure, economists have focused on real GDP per person as a key measure of a country's living standard and stage of economic development. As discussed in Chapter 18, real GDP per person is positively related to a number of pertinent variables, such as life expectancy, infant health, and literacy. During the 19th century, the annual percentage change in real GDP per person began to increase in a number of industrializing countries, and during the latter half of the 20th century the rate of economic growth increased again. As a result of the power of compound interest, real GDP in these countries is anywhere from 4 to 25 times greater than it was a century ago. However, since 1973 there has been a slowdown in the growth rates that has puzzled economists and policymakers alike.

> **Note:** Since the mid-1990s growth rates in real GDP have begun to accelerate again in many countries, giving some analysts hope that the period of slow down is over while others have gone further declaring a "new economy."

Learning Objective 2: Define compound interest and explain the effects of compound interest.

The increases in the growth rates of real GDP during the last half of the 20th century were relatively small in comparison to the previous 80 years, but the power of compound interest resulted in large changes in real GDP over time. **Compound interest** is the payment of interest not only on the original deposit, but also on all previously accumulated interest. This is distinguished from simple interest in which interest is paid only on the original deposit. When interest is compounded, small differences in interest rates or growth rates matter a lot. As in the case of the industrializing countries during the late 19th and 20th centuries, relatively small differences in growth rates, among the countries and during different time periods, ultimately produced very different living standards.

> **Note:** One way of grasping the power of compound interest is to apply what is often referred to as the "rule of 72." The rule of 72 is a quick way of estimating how long it will take for a country's real GDP to double as a result of a country's economic growth. For example, if GDP is growing at an average annual rate of two percent, by dividing 2 into 72 we find that the GDP will double in approximately 36 years. If growth increases to 3 percent, GDP will double in only 24 years.

Learning Objective 3: Discuss the relationship of real GDP per person to average labor productivity and share of working population.

Real GDP per person can be expressed as the product of two terms: average labor productivity and the share of the population that is working. Real GDP per person can only grow if there is growth in worker productivity and/or the fraction of the population that is employed. In the United States, for example, during 1960-99 the fraction of the population employed increased as women entered the labor force in greater proportions, and as the coming of age of the "baby boomers" increased the share of the population that was of working age. This contributed to the increased growth in real GDP per capita in the United States during that time. In the long run, however, it is unlikely that this trend will continue as demographic changes take place. Average labor productivity is, therefore, the more important determinant of increases in living standards in the long run. In simple terms, the more people produce, the more they can consume.

Learning Objective 4: Discuss the determinants of average labor productivity.
There are six factors that appear to account for the major differences in average labor productivity between countries and between generations. Human capital, i.e., the talents, education, training and skills of workers, is the *first* factor that affects average labor productivity. In general, people acquire additional education and skills when the difference in the additional wages paid (marginal benefit) to skilled workers is greater than the marginal cost of acquiring the skills. A *second* determinant of average labor productivity is physical capital, machines, equipment, and buildings. More capital generally increases average labor productivity. There are, however, **diminishing returns to capital** (i.e., if the amount of labor and other inputs employed is held constant, then the greater the amount of capital already in use, the less an additional unit of capital adds to production).

Note: Diminishing returns to capital is an illustration of the principle of increasing opportunity cost, or the low-hanging fruit principle. Capital will first be applied to the most productive activities available, thus, as additional capital is applied the marginal return will eventually begin to decline.

The *third* determinant of average labor productivity is the availability of land and other resources. In general, an abundance of natural resources increases the productivity of the workers who use them. Because resources can be obtained through trade, countries need not possess large quantities of them within their own borders to achieve economic growth. A *fourth* determinant is technology. A country's ability to develop and apply new, more productive, technologies will increase its workers' productivity.

Note: Most economists would probably agree that new technologies are the single most important source of productivity improvements. Although a stable political and legal environment may be considered a prerequisite for a country to take advantage of the other five source of productivity improvements.

Entrepreneurship and management are a *fifth* determinant of average labor productivity. **Entrepreneurs** are people who create new enterprises and who are critical to the introduction of new technologies into the production of goods and services. Managers also play an important role in determining average labor productivity as they work to introduce new technologies to better satisfy customers, organize production, obtain financing, assign workers to jobs, and motivate them to work hard and effectively. Government, a *sixth* determinant, also has a role to play in fostering improved productivity. A key contribution of government is to provide a political and legal environment that encourages people to behave in economically productive ways. A stable government and well-defined property rights and free markets are important determinants of a nation's average labor productivity.

Learning Objective 5: Identify the costs of economic growth.

While economic growth provides substantial benefits to society, it is not without costs. The high rate of investment in new physical and human capital requires that people save and, thus, consume less in the present. Also, reduced leisure time and, possibly, reduced workers' health and safety must be sacrificed in the present for workers to acquire the education and skills to build the capital infrastructure.

> **Note**: The fact that a higher living standard tomorrow must be purchased at the cost of current sacrifices is an example of the scarcity principle. The cost-benefit principle suggests that a nation should pursue additional growth only if the marginal benefits outweigh the marginal costs.

Learning Objective 6: Discuss potential government policies that may promote economic growth.

If a society decides to try to increase its rate of economic growth, policymakers can help to achieve the goal by providing education and training programs or by subsidizing the provision of such programs by the private sector. In addition, governments can encourage high rates of saving and investment in the private sector through tax incentives. Governments can also directly contribute to capital formation through public investment in infrastructure. Government financing of research and development activities, especially in the area of basic scientific knowledge, and sharing the fruits of applied research in military and space applications can promote a higher rate of economic growth. Government also plays an essential role in providing the framework within which the private sector can operate productively, an area in which the poorest countries of the world lack adequate structural macroeconomic policies.

Learning Objective 7: Identify the issues raised in *The Limits to Growth*.

While economic growth accelerated during the 19th and 20th centuries, an influential book, *The Limits to Growth*, published in 1972 reported the results of computer simulations that suggested continued growth would deplete natural resources, drinkable water, and breathable air. Critics of the limits to growth thesis point out that its underlying assumption is that growth implies producing more of the same type of goods. A second criticism is that it overlooks the fact that increased wealth expands a society's capacity to safeguard the environment. Additionally, it is argued that markets and government action can deal with the depletion of natural resources through new sources and conservation. Despite these shortcomings of the "limits to growth" perspective, most economists would agree that not all the problems created by economic growth can be dealt with effectively. Global environmental pollution will remain a problem unless international mechanisms are developed to deal with them. In particular, given that the relationship between pollution and real GDP per person is shaped like an inverted **U**, it is likely that as poorer countries become middle-income countries they will continue to pollute more until they become sufficiently wealthy to have the luxury of a clean environment.

III. Self-Test

Key Terms
Match the term in the right-hand column with the appropriate definitions in the left-hand column by placing the letter of the term in the blank in front of its definition. (Answers are given at the end of the chapter.)

1. _____ If the amount of labor and other inputs employed is held constant, then the greater the amount of capital already in use, the less an additional unit of capital adds to production.

a. compound interest

2. _____ People who create new economic enterprises.

b. diminishing returns to capital

3. _____ The payment of interest not only on the original deposit but on all previously accumulated interest.

c. entrepreneurs

Multiple-Choice Questions
Circle the letter that corresponds to the best answer. (Answers are given at the end of the chapter.)

1. The rate of growth in real GDP per person in the United States, Japan, Canada, Australia, and the major European economies was highest during the period of
   A. 1870-1998.
   B. 1950-1998.
   C. 1973-1979.
   D. 1979-1997.
   E. 1960-1973.

2. Compound interest differs from simple interest in that compound interest is interest paid on
   A. the original deposit only, whereas simple interest is interest paid on not only the original deposit but also on all previously accumulated interest.
   B. all previously accumulated interest, whereas simple interest is interest paid on not only the original deposit but also on all previously accumulated interest.
   C. the original deposit only, whereas simple interest is interest paid only on all previously accumulated interest.
   D. the original deposit and on all previously accumulated interest, whereas simple interest is interest paid on all previously accumulated interest .
   E. the original deposit and on all previously accumulated interest, whereas simple interest is interest paid on the original deposit only.

3. If on the day you were born, your parents deposited $1,000 into a savings account that would earn an annual compound interest rate of 5 percent, what would the value of the account be on your 20th birthday?
   A. $1,100.00
   B. $2,653.30
   C. $3,325,256.73
   D. $1,500.00

E. $1,050.00

4. The increase in average labor productivity is important to the economy because
    A. without it, real GDP per person cannot increase.
    B. without it, real GDP per person must decrease.
    C. it is a key to improving living standards in the long run.
    D. the fraction of the total population that is employed is constant over time and, thus, real GDP per person is solely dependent upon average labor productivity.
    E. it implies more resources are being employed to produce less output.

5. International data on the relationship between the amount of capital per worker and average labor productivity indicate that there is a
    A. positive relationship between the two variables.
    B. negative relationship between the two variables.
    C. no relationship between the two variables.
    D. positive relationship between the two variables for some countries, but a negative relationship between the two variables for other countries.
    E. positive relationship between the two variables for some countries, but no relationship between the two variables for other countries.

6. An abundance of natural resources, such as arable land, raw materials, and energy,
    A. within a country's borders is necessary to achieve economic growth.
    B. increases the productivity of workers who use them.
    C. results in economic growth only if the population increases at least as rapidly.
    D. results in economic growth only if an economy obtains them through international trade.
    E. seldom contribute to economic growth, as measured by percentage increases in real GDP per person.

7. The investment in human capital that contributed to the rapid economic recovery in Germany and Japan after World War II was mainly achieved through
    A. a superior system of higher education.
    B. public education.
    C. an apprentice system and on-the-job training.
    D. subsidies provided by the U.S.-funded Marshall Plan.
    E. a large wage differential paid to skilled versus unskilled workers.

8. The faster the rate of technological change, the
    A. lower the rate of growth in productivity.
    B. lower the rate of economic growth.
    C. higher the rate of unemployment.
    D. higher the rate of productivity.
    E. higher the rate of capital accumulation.

9. For a given number of workers, as the amount of capital is increased, output will
    A. increase at a diminishing rate.
    B. increase at an increasing rate.

    C. increase at a constant rate.

    D. decrease at a diminishing rate.

    E. decrease at an increasing rate.

10. Entrepreneurship is

    A. easy to teach in schools and colleges.

    B. not affected by government policies.

    C. more important than management in determining average labor productivity.

    D. mainly affected by individual factors rather than sociological factors.

    E. believed to have been largely absent in medieval China.

11. Which of the following contributed to the worldwide slowdown in productivity since 1973?

    A. the increase in the price of oil that followed the Arab-Israeli war of 1973

    B. the decline in the quality of public education

    C. the improvement in the measurement of productivity growth

    D. a dearth of technological innovations during the 1970s

    E. an increase in technological innovations during the 1970s

12. The scarcity principle implies that the cost of a higher economic growth rate is

    A. less future capital accumulation.

    B. less current consumption.

    C. greater future capital consumption.

    D. greater current consumption.

    E. greater future consumption.

13. The cost-benefit principle suggests that higher economic growth

    A. is always desirable.

    B. is seldom desirable.

    C. should be pursued only if the marginal benefits outweigh the marginal costs.

    D. should be pursued only if the marginal costs outweigh the marginal benefits.

    E. should be pursued only if the marginal benefits equal the marginal costs.

14. Most countries provide their citizens free public education through high school because

    A. the supply curve for education does not include all the social benefits of education.

    B. a market in equilibrium exploits all the gains achievable from collective action.

    C. the demand curve for education does not include all the social benefits of education.

    D. educational vouchers that help citizens purchase educational services in the private sector have not proven to increase human capital.

    E. direct government control over the standards and quality of education is necessary to increase human capital.

15. The U. S. government has promoted saving or investment in the economy by

    A. increasing the tax rates on Individual Retirement Accounts (IRAs).

    B. providing subsidies to the private sector to build infrastructure.

    C. reducing the amount of public investment in government-owned capital.

    D. providing funding during the early stages of the development of the internet.

E. eliminating all taxes on Individual Retirement Accounts (IRAs).

16. In order to increase their rate of economic growth, most poor countries need to
    A. establish political stability and the rule of law.
    B. obtain greater financial support from the rich countries.
    C. extract more of the natural resources that lie within their borders.
    D. maintain the structural macroeconomic policies that they began to implement after World War II.
    E. increase regulation of private sector monopolies.

17. The general thesis of the book, *The Limits to Growth*, is that continued pursuit of economic growth will soon
    A. cease when all the workers are employed.
    B. consume all available natural resources, drinkable water, and breathable air.
    C. cause the principle of scarcity to no longer be an issue.
    D. increase the living standard of the poorest nations to that of the richest nations.
    E. limit our desire to increase the production of goods and services.

18. Critics of the "limits to growth" thesis argue that
    A. economic growth will always take the form of more of what we have now, rather than newer, better, and cleaner goods and services.
    B. the market is not capable of adjusting to shortages of resources.
    C. clean air and water is a luxury good and the more economically developed a country becomes the easier it will be to keep the environment clean.
    D. government action spurred by political pressure is the best way to avoid the depletion of natural resources and pollution of the environment that results from economic growth.
    E. all the problems created by economic growth can be dealt with effectively through the market or the political process.

19. One criticism of the "limits to growth" thesis is that the market can deal with shortages of natural resources that may result from economic growth through price changes that induce
    A. consumers to consume more and suppliers to produce less of the resources.
    B. consumers to consume less and suppliers to produce more of the resources.
    C. a slowdown in the rate of economic growth.
    D. government actions to allocate public funds to preserve open space and reduce air pollution.
    E. an optimal level of environmental quality on a global scale.

20. Empirical studies show that the relationship between pollution and real GDP per person takes the shape of an inverted **U**. This suggests that as countries move from very low levels of real GDP per person the level of pollution
    A. tends to continuously worsen.
    B. tends to continuously improve.
    C. improves, but from middle-income to high-income levels pollution worsens.
    D. worsens, but from middle-income to high-income levels pollution improves.
    E. worsens at middle-income levels, but improves at high-income levels.

Short Answer Problems
(Answers and solutions are given at the end of the chapter.)

1. Compounding Economic Growth Rates
The table below shows the output per person for selected countries in 1998 and the economic growth rates of the countries for 1990-98. Use the data in the table to answer the following questions.

Country	1998 GNP per capita[1]	1990 – 1998 Growth Rate	2008 GNP per capita
Canada	$24,050	2.2%	
France	22,320	1.5%	
Germany	20,810	1.6%	
Italy	20,200	1.2%	
Mexico	8,190	2.5%	
New Zealand	15,840	3.2%	

Source: *World Development Report, 1999/2000*, Tables 1 and 11.
[1] Calculated in 1998 dollars and using the purchasing power parity method to adjust the value of output across countries.

A. Assuming that each country's economy continues to grow at the same rate that it did during 1990-98, complete column 4 of the table by calculating the GNP per capita (person) for 2008.

B. On the graph below, plot the level of GNP per capita for the remaining countries for 10, 20, 50, and 100 years later, assuming a compound growth rate equal to that of 1990-98,

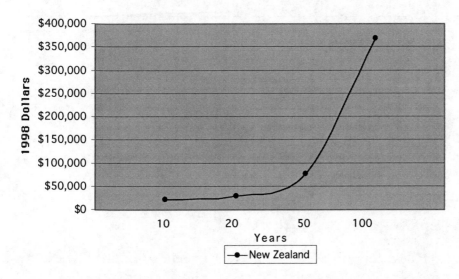

C. Approximately how many decades would it take for New Zealand's output per person to equal that of Canada's output per person? _____ decades.

D. Approximately how many decades would it take for Germany's output per person to equal that of France's output per person? _____ decades.

E. Approximately how many decades would it take for Mexico's output per person to equal that of Italy's output per person? _____ decades.

2. Why Nations Become Rich

This problem will help you understand the relationship between how much workers produce, how many people are working, and the quantity of goods and services available to consume. The following table is compiled from data published by the U.S. Department of Labor's Bureau of Labor Statistics/Office of Productivity and Technology. All data are for 1998 and the Real GDP and productivity are measured in 1998 dollars.

Country	Real GDP per person	Average Labor Productivity	Share of the population Employed
United States		$65,888	49.2
Canada	$25,496		47.5
France	$22,255	$56,722	
Japan	$24,170		51.2
Norway		$54,007	51.1

A. Complete the table above by calculating the value of real GDP per person for the United States and Norway, average labor productivity for Canada and Japan, and the share of the population employed in France during 1998.

B. The data indicate that workers in France produce considerable more output per year than do the workers in Norway, yet the average Norwegian has a higher standard of living. Explain why.

_____

C. A larger share of the population in Japan is employed than in the United States, yet the average American has a higher standard of living than the Japanese do. Explain why.

_____

D. The population in Japan is aging faster than the population in Canada and, thus, by the early 21st century the share of the population employed in Japan will decline as the elderly retire. If the share of the population employed in Japan falls to the level of Canada, which country would have the higher real GDP per capita, assuming no other changes? _____
Explain your answer. _____

IV. Economic Naturalist Application

Economic Naturalist 7.5 discusses the relationship between a country's level of income (real GDP per person) and the amount of air pollution in the country. The following table shows the classification by level of Real GDP per person of a limited number of countries in the *World Development Report 1999/2000*, and the graph shows the empirical relationship between air pollution and Real GDP per person.

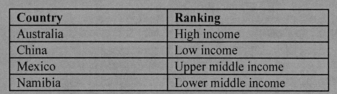

Country	Ranking
Australia	High income
China	Low income
Mexico	Upper middle income
Namibia	Lower middle income

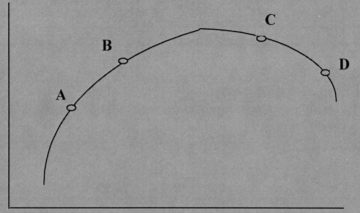

Identify each of the four countries listed in the table with one of the lettered points on the inverted U-shaped curve on the following graph. If the level of real GDP per person in Mexico increases so that it moves up to the next classification in future World Development Reports, will the amount of pollution likely increase or decrease? If the level of real GDP per person in China increases so that it moves up to the next classification in future World Development Reports, will the amount of pollution likely increase or decrease?

V. Go to the Web: Graphing Exercises Using Interactive Graphs

Average Labor Productivity vs. Share of Population Working

In the text, the authors note that, Output per person = average labor productivity (Y/N) x share of population employed (N/POP). How do the long-run effects on output per person resulting from changes in average labor productivity compare to those resulting from increases in the share of the population that is working?
Answer:

To review the answer to this question and learn more about the use of economic theory to analyze macroeconomic issues, please go to the Electronic Learning Session in the Student Center at the Frank/Bernanke web site: http://www.mhhe.com/economics/frankbernanke2.

VI. Self-Test Solutions

Key Terms
1. b
2. c
3. a

Multiple-Choice Questions
1. E Compare the growth rates for each of these periods in Tables 7.1 and 7.3
2. D
3. B $1,000 x 1.05^{20} = $2,653.30
4. C
5. A See Figure 7.4
6. B
7. C See Economic Naturalist 7.1
8. D
9. A
10. E
11. D
12. B
13. C
14. C
15. D
16. A
17. B

1. C
2. B
3. E

Short Answer Problems

1.

A.

Country	1998 GNP per capita	2008 GNP	2018 GNP
Canada	$24,050.00	$29,896.75	$37,164.90
France	$22,320.00	$25,903.27	$30,061.80
Germany	$20,810.00	$24,389.85	$28,585.53
Italy	$20,200.00	$22,759.17	$25,642.57
Mexico	$8,190.00	$10,483.89	$13,420.27
New Zealand	$15,840.00	$21,704.62	$29,740.56

B.

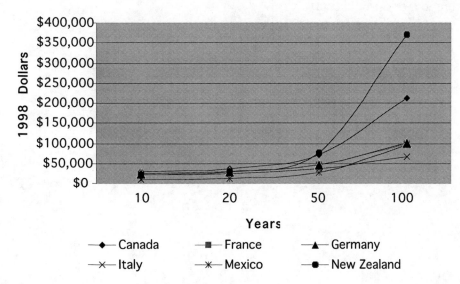

C. 5

D. 5

E. 6

2.

A.

Country	Real GDP per person	Average Labor Productivity	Share of the population Employed
US	$32,413	$65,888	49.2
Canada	$25,496	$53,702	47.5
France	$22,255	$56,722	39.2
Japan	$24,170	$47,232	51.2
Norway	$27,581	$54,007	51.1

B. Because a larger share of the population is employed in Norway than is employed in France, the average person in Norway has a higher standard of living than the French.

C. The average labor productivity in the United States is higher than that of Japan, and, thus, despite the fact that a smaller share of the population is employed in the U.S., its citizens have a higher standard of living.

D. Canada. If the share of the population employed in Japan declines to that of Canada, the standard of living for the average Canadian will be higher than that of the average Japanese because of its higher average labor productivity.

Chapter 10
Money, Prices, and the Federal Reserve

I. Pretest: What Do You Really Know?

Circle the letter that corresponds to the best answer. (Answers appear immediately after the final question).

1. Money is
   A. the same as income.
   B. all financial assets.
   C. any asset used to make purchases.
   D. the sum of assets minus debts.
   E. the market value of all final goods and services produced in a country in a year.

2. The functions of money include as a
   A. medium of exchange, diversification of risk, and store of value.
   B. medium of exchange, unit of value, and store of account.
   C. medium of value, unit of exchange, and store of account.
   D. medium of account, store of value, and unit of exchange.
   E. medium of exchange, unit of account, and store of value.

3. M1 consists of
   A. currency and balances held in checking accounts.
   B. currency outstanding and balances held in checking accounts.
   C. M2 plus savings deposits, small-denomination time deposits, and money market mutual funds.
   D. currency outstanding, balances in checking accounts plus savings deposits, small-denomination time deposits, and money market mutual funds.
   E. M2 minus balances in checking accounts, savings deposits, small-denomination time deposits, and money market mutual funds.

4. Banks reserves are
   A. cash or similar assets held for the purpose of meeting depositor withdrawals and payments.
   B. cash or similar assets held for the purpose of insuring bank deposits.
   C. cash or similar assets held for the purpose of making loans.

D. cash or similar assets held for the purpose of ensuring that loans are repaid and depositors' funds are not depleted.

E. cash or similar assets held for the purpose of facilitating monetary policy.

5. The two main responsibilities of the Federal Reserve System are to _____ and to _____.

    A. apprehend counterfeiters; regulate the stock market

    B. enable banks to make affordable mortgages; control the exchange rate of the U.S. dollar

    C. insure bank deposits; print currency

    D. conduct monetary policy; oversee financial markets

    E. collect taxes; pay the government's expenses

6. The most important, most convenient, and most flexible way in which the Federal Reserve affects the supply of bank reserves is by

    A. conducting open-market operations.

    B. changing the Federal Reserve discount rate.

    C. changing bank reserve requirement ratios.

    D. changing interest rates.

    E. conducting bank examinations.

7. The interest rate the Federal Reserve charges commercial banks to borrow reserves is called the _____ rate.

    A. Fed funds

    B. prime

    C. discount

    D. Federal

    E. U.S. interest

8. Deposit insurance is a system in which the government guarantees that

    A. depositors will not lose any money even if their bank goes bankrupt.

    B. people can have deposits at commercial banks.

    C. commercial banks will not go bankrupt.

    D. depositors of commercial banks can obtain low-cost life insurance.

    E. commercial banks will not lose any deposits.

9. If the Federal Reserve wants to decrease the money supply, it will

    A. decrease reserve requirements.

    B. decrease the discount rate.

    C. conduct open-market purchases.

    D. conduct open-market sales.

    E. decrease interest rates.

10. In the long run, a higher rate of growth in the money supply will cause a higher rate
    of inflation
    A. if the velocity of money increases.
    B. because the larger amount of money in circulation will allow people to bid up the
       prices of goods and services.
    C. because the higher velocity of money will allow people to bid up the prices of
       goods and services.
    D. because the larger quantity of transactions will allow people to bid up the prices of
       goods and services.
    E. if the velocity of money increases and the quantity of transactions is constant.

Solutions and Feedback to Pretest
For each question you incorrectly answered, we strongly recommend taking the time to
review the appropriate material before continuing. In the table below, the relevant
textbook pages are listed for each question as well as the pertinent Learning Objective
from the following Key Point Review.

Correct Answer	Textbook Page Numbers	Learning Objective
1. C	p. 260	1
2. E	pp. 260 - 61	2
3. B	p. 262	3
4. A	p. 264	4
5. D	p. 268	7
6. A	pp. 270 - 71	6
7. C	p. 271	6
8. A	pp. 271 - 74	7
9. D	pp. 270 - 71	6
10. B	pp. 275 - 76	8

II. Key Point Review

In this chapter the role of money in modern economies is discussed, including why
money is important, how it is measured, and how it is created. In addition, the role of the
central bank is introduced along with some of the monetary policy tools at its disposal.

Learning Objective 1: Define money and barter.
Money is any asset that can be used in making purchases. Without money, all economic
transactions would have to be in the form of **barter**, that is, the direct trade of goods and
services for other goods and services. Barter is inefficient because it requires that both
parties to a trade have something the other party wants, a so-called double coincidence of
wants. Money facilitates more efficient transactions and permits individuals to specialize
in producing particular goods and services.

Learning Objective 2: Define the three functions of money.
Money has three principal uses: it serves as a medium of exchange, a unit of account, and a store of value. Money serves as a **medium of exchange** when it is used to purchase goods and services. As a **unit of account**, money is the basic yardstick for measuring economic value. As a **store of value** money serves as a means of holding wealth.

> **Note:** The store of value function of money is undermined by inflation because inflation erodes the purchasing power of money. When you hold some of your wealth in the form of money and the economy experiences inflation, over time what you can purchase with those dollars decreases. It makes sense then that, as the purchasing power of your money decreases, you will choose to hold less of your wealth in the form of money (and, thus, more of your wealth in some other form, e.g., land). During periods of hyperinflation (rapidly escalating inflation), the medium of exchange function of money can also be undermined. That is, people will prefer not to accept money in exchange for goods and services, may revert to a barter system, or may give preference to some nondomestic currencies (e.g., dollars rather than rubles).

Learning Objective 3: Define the amount of M1 and M2.
When measuring the quantity of money in the economy, economists vary as to how they define the concept of money. The narrowest definition of the amount of money in the United States is called **M1**, the sum of currency outstanding and balances held in checking accounts. A broader measure of the money supply is **M2**, which includes all the assets in M1 plus savings deposits, small-denomination time deposits, and money market mutual funds. Because the definition of the money supply includes both currency and bank deposits, the amount of money is the economy depends in part on the behavior of commercial banks and their depositors. When households or businesses deposit currency into a bank, the currency becomes a part of the bank reserves.

> **Hint:** Because the money measures are cumulative, when calculating M2 be sure to remember to begin with the value of M1 (or the amounts of the components that make of M1) before adding in the value of the non-M1 components.

Learning Objective 4: Define bank reserves, 100% reserve banking, reserve/deposit ratio, and fractional reserve banking system.
Bank reserves are cash or similar assets held by commercial banks for the purpose of meeting depositor withdrawals and payments. When banks must keep bank reserves equal to the amount of their deposits, it is referred to as a **100% reserve banking system**. If banks can maintain a **reserve/deposit ratio** (bank reserves divided by deposits) of less than 100%, then it is referred to as a **fractional-reserve banking**

system. In a fractional-reserve banking system the amount of the money supply is expanded when banks make loans in the form of new deposits.

Learning Objective 5: Define the Federal Reserve System, Board of Governors, and Federal Open-Market Committee and discuss the structure of each component of the Fed.

The **Federal Reserve System**, often called the Fed, is the central bank of the United States and is responsible for monetary policy, as well as oversight and regulation of financial markets. The leadership of the Fed is provided by its **Board of Governors**, consisting of seven members appointed by the President to staggered fourteen-year terms. Decisions about monetary policy are made by the **Federal Open Market Committee (FOMC)**, which is made up of the seven members of the Board of Governors, the President of the Federal Reserve Bank of New York, and four of the presidents of the other Federal Reserve Banks. The Fed's primary responsibility is making monetary policy, which involves decisions about the appropriate size of the nation's money supply. The Fed controls the money supply indirectly by changing the amount of reserves held by commercial banks. The Fed affects the amount of reserves through open-market operations, discount window lending, and changing reserve requirements.

Learning Objective 6: Explain how the Fed uses the tools of monetary policy to change the amount of bank reserves and the money supply.

Open-market operations, the most important tool of monetary policy, include **open-market purchases** of government bonds from the public for the purpose of increasing the supply of banks reserves and the money supply, and **open-market sales** of government bonds to the public for the purpose of reducing bank reserves and the money supply. **Discount window lending** of reserves by the Fed to commercial banks is the second tool the Fed uses to affect bank reserves. When the Fed lends reserves, the quantity of reserves in the banking system is directly increased and, ultimately, bank deposits and the money supply can increase. The **discount rate** is the interest rate the Fed charges commercial banks to borrow reserves. The Fed can also affect the amount of reserves in the banking system by changing the reserve requirements. **Reserve requirements** are the minimum values of the ratio of bank reserves to bank deposits that commercial banks are allowed to maintain. Although the Fed has the authority to change reserve requirements to affect the money supply, it seldom does.

Note: It is often observed that the Fed will announce an increase (or decrease) in the discount rate and this is followed by an increase (or decrease) in market interest rates. This can lead to the erroneously conclusion that the Fed changed market interest rates by changing the discount rate. The real cause of the change in market interest rates is much more likely to be open-market operations that are simultaneously carried out by the Fed. Because the open-market operations result in a change in bank reserves, market interest rates are affected. Open-market operations, however, are a much less visible policy and, thus, many observers mistakenly attribute the changes in market interest rates to the more visible discount rate policy changes.

Learning Objective 7: Explain the Fed's role in stabilizing financial markets.
Besides controlling the money supply, the Fed has the responsibility (along with other government agencies) of ensuring that financial markets operate smoothly. Historically, in the United States, banking panics were the most disruptive type of recurrent financial crisis. A banking panic is an episode in which depositors, spurred by news or rumors of the imminent bankruptcy of one or more banks, rush to withdraw their deposits from the banking system. The Fed, established in 1913 in response to a particularly severe banking panic in 1907, was given the power to supervise and regulate banks to create greater confidence in banks, and was allowed to lend cash to banks to help them meet withdrawals during a bank panic. Following the creation of the Fed there were no bank panics until 1930. During 1930-33, however, the United States experienced the worst and most protracted series of bank panics in its history. The inability of the Fed to stop the bank panics of the 1930s caused Congress to institute a system of deposit insurance. Under a system of deposit insurance, the government guarantees depositors that they will get their money back even if the bank goes bankrupt, eliminating the incentive of depositors to withdraw their deposits when rumors of financial trouble are circulating.

Learning Objective 8: Explain the relationship between money and prices in the long run.
In the long run, the rate of growth of the money supply and the inflation rate are positively related. That is, a higher rate of growth in the money supply will cause a higher rate of inflation because the larger amount of money in circulation will allow people to bid up the prices of goods and services. Velocity measures the speed at which money circulates and is calculated as the value of transactions (or nominal GDP) divided by the supply of money. The definition of velocity can be rewritten as the quantity equation, or $M \times V = P \times Y$. The quantity equation shows that, if velocity and output are constant, a given percentage increase in the money supply will lead to the same percentage increase in the price level.

Hint: The key to understanding the last sentence in the above paragraph is to recognize that the quantity equation refers to **amounts** of money supply and price **level**, while the last sentence refers to a **change** in the money supply and the **change** in the price level.

I. Self-Test

Key Terms
Match the term in the right-hand column with the appropriate definitions in the left-hand column by placing the letter of the term in the blank in front of its definition. (Answers are given at the end of the chapter.)

1. _____ A basic measure of economic value.   a. bank reserves
2. _____ Any asset that can be used in making purchases.   b. banking panic
3. _____ Bank reserves divided by deposits.   c. barter

4. ____ The sum of currency outstanding and balances held in checking accounts.

5. ____ A situation in which banks' reserves equal 100 percent of their deposits.

6. ____ Cash or similar assets held by commercial banks for the purpose of meeting depositor withdrawals and payments.

7. ____ An asset used in purchasing goods and services.

8. ____ An asset that serves as a means of holding wealth.

9. ____ All the assets in M1 plus some additional assets that are usable in making payments but at greater cost or inconvenience than currency or checks.

10.____ The direct trade of goods or services for other goods or services.

11.____ The leadership of the Fed, consisting of seven governors appointed by the President to staggered 14-year terms.

12.____ A banking system in which bank reserves are less than deposits so that the reserve-deposit ratio is less than 100 percent.

13.____ The committee that makes decisions concerning monetary policy.

14.____ The central bank of the United States.

15.____ Open-market purchases and open-market sales.

16.____ The lending of reserves by the Federal Reserve to commercial banks.

17.____ A system under which the government guarantees that depositors will not lose any money even if their bank goes bankrupt.

18.____ The sale by the Fed of government bonds to the public for the purpose of reducing bank reserves and the money supply.

19.____ A measure of the speed at which money circulates.

20.____ The minimum values of the ratio of bank reserves to bank deposits that commercial banks are allowed to maintain.

21.____ Money times velocity equals nominal GDP.

22.____ An episode in which depositors, spurred by news or rumors of the imminent bankruptcy of one or more banks, rush to withdraw their deposits from the banking system.

23.____ The purchase of government bonds from the public by the Fed for the purpose of increasing the supply of bank reserves and the money supply.

24.____ The interest rate that the Fed charges commercial banks to borrow reserves.

d. Board of Governors

e. deposit insurance

f. discount rate

g. discount window lending

h. Federal Open-Market Committee (or FOMC)

i. Federal Reserve System (or Fed)

j. fractional-reserve banking system

k. M1

l. M2

m. medium of exchange

n. money

o. 100 percent reserves banking

p. open-market operations

q. open-market purchases

r. open-market sale

s. quantity equation

t. reserve requirements

u. reserve-deposit ratio

v. store of value

w. unit of account

x. velocity

Multiple-Choice Questions
Circle the letter that corresponds to the best answer. (Answers are given at the end of the chapter.)

1. Double coincidence of wants is avoided if money is used as a
   A. medium of exchange.
   B. measure of value.
   C. standard of deferred payment.
   D. store of value.
   E. tool of monetary policy.

2. Money serves as a basic yardstick for measuring economic value (i.e., a unit of account), allowing
   A. people to hold their wealth in a liquid form.
   B. governments to restrict the issuance of private monies.
   C. easy comparison of the relative prices of goods and services.
   D. goods and services to be exchanged with a double coincidence of wants.
   E. private money to be issued for local use.

3. In the United States, money is issued
   A. only by the Fed.
   B. by the Fed and all commercial banks.
   C. mainly by the Fed, but also privately in some communities.
   D. once per year by the Fed.
   E. by the U.S. Congress

4. M1 differs from M2 in that
   A. M1 includes currency and balances held in checking accounts, which are not included in M2.
   B. M2 includes savings deposits, small-denomination time deposits, and money market mutual funds, which are not included in M1
   C. M2 includes small savings accounts, large time deposits, and money market mutual funds, which are not included in M1.
   D. M1 is a broader measure of the money supply than M2.
   E. the assets in M2 are more liquid than the assets in M1.

5. The difference between a fractional-reserve banking system and a 100 percent reserve banking system is that a fractional-reserve banking system
   A. only allows banks to lend a fraction of their reserves, whereas a 100 percent banking system allows banks to lend 100 percent of their reserves.
   B. only allows the money supply to increase by a fraction of banks' reserves, whereas a 100 percent banking system allows the money supply to increase by 100 percent of their reserves.
   C. does not allow banks to lend their reserves, but a 100 percent reserve banking system does allow banks to lend their reserves.

D. allows banks to lend some of their reserves, but a 100 percent reserve banking system does not allow banks to lend any of their reserves.

E. does not allow for growth in the money supply through bank lending, while a 100 percent reserve banking system does allow for growth in the money supply through bank lending.

6. When a bank makes a loan by crediting the borrower's checking account balance with an amount equal to the loan
    A. money is created.
    B. the bank gains new reserves.
    C. the bank immediately loses reserves.
    D. money is destroyed.
    E. the Fed has made an open-market purchase.

7. If a bank's desired reserve/deposit ratio is .33 and it has deposit liabilities of $100 million and reserves of $50 million, it
    A. has too few reserves and will reduce its lending.
    B. has too many reserves and will increase its lending.
    C. has the correct amount of reserves and outstanding loans.
    D. should increase the amount of its reserves.
    E. should decrease the amount of its reserves.

8. If the reserve/deposit ratio is .25 and the banking system receives an additional $10 million in reserves, bank deposits can increase by a maximum of
    A. $10 million.
    B. $250 million.
    C. $400 million.
    D. $4 million.
    E. $40 million.

9. Decisions about the United States' monetary policy are made by the
    A. U.S. Congress.
    B. President of the United States.
    C. Fed's Board of Governors.
    D. Federal Open-Market Committee (FOMC).
    E. 12 presidents of the regional Federal Reserve Banks.

10. The most important tool of monetary policy is
    A. reserve requirement ratios.
    B. the discount rate.
    C. open-market operations.
    D. the minimum net worth required of banks.
    E. market interest rates.

11. When the Fed sells government securities, the banks'
    A. reserves will increase and lending will expand, causing an increase in the money supply.
    B. reserves will decrease and lending will contract, causing a decrease in the money supply.
    C. reserve requirements will increase and lending will contract, causing a decrease in the money supply.
    D. reserves/deposit ratio will increase and lending will expand, causing an increase in the money supply.
    E. reserves/deposit ratio will decrease and lending will contract, causing an increase in the money supply.

12. An open-market purchase of government securities by the Fed will
    A. increase bank reserves, and the money supply will increase.
    B. decrease bank reserves, and the money supply will increase.
    C. increase bank reserves, and the money supply will decrease.
    D. decrease bank reserves, and the money supply will decrease.
    E. increase bank reserves, and the money supply will not change.

13. When banks borrow funds via the Fed's discount window
    A. interest rates rise.
    B. the reserve/deposit ratio falls.
    C. bank reserves are increased and, ultimately, bank deposits and the money supply increase.
    D. bank reserves are decreased and, ultimately, bank deposits and the money supply increase.
    E. bank reserves are increased and, ultimately, bank deposits and the money supply decrease.

14. When an individual deposits currency into a checking account
    A. bank reserves increase, which allows banks to lend more and, ultimately, increases the money supply.
    B. bank reserves decrease, which reduces the amount banks can lend thereby reducing the growth of the money supply.
    C. bank reserves are unchanged.
    D. bank reserves decrease, which increases the amount banks can lend, thereby increasing the growth of the money supply.
    E. bank reserves increase, which reduces the amount banks can lend, thereby reducing the growth of the money supply.

15. Deposit insurance for banks
    A. helped the Fed combat the bank panics of 1930-33.
    B. was first legislated by the Federal Reserve Bank Act of 1913.
    C. may induce the managers of banks to take more risks.
    D. guarantees the interest payments on depositors' checking accounts.
    E. is a perfect solution to the problem of bank panics.

16. Holding money as a store of wealth has the advantage of being useful as a medium of exchange and being anonymous. The disadvantages of holding your wealth in the form of currency are that it
    A. may be stolen or lost, and people may think you're a smuggler or drug dealer.
    B. is difficult to trace and may be lost or stolen.
    C. may be lost or stolen and usually pays no interest.
    D. pays no interest and is difficult to trace.
    E. pays no interest and people may think you're a smuggler or drug dealer.

17. During the bank panic of 1930-33, the public withdrew deposits from the bank preferring to hold currency. As a result,
    A. bank reserves decreased but were offset by an equal increase in currency, with no net effect on the money supply.
    B. bank reserves increased by less than the increase in currency, causing the money supply to decrease.
    C. bank reserves decreased by more than the increase in currency, causing the money supply to decrease.
    D. bank reserves decreased by less than the increase in currency, causing the money supply to increase.
    E. bank reserves decreased by an amount equal to the increase in currency, causing the money supply to decrease.

18. From a macroeconomic perspective, a major reason that control of the supply of money is important is that,
    A. in the long run, the higher the rate of inflation, the higher the rate of growth of the money supply.
    B. in the long run, the higher the rate of growth of the money supply, the higher the rate of inflation.
    C. in the short run, the higher the rate of growth of the money supply, the higher the rate of inflation.
    D. in the long run, the lower the rate of growth of the money supply, the higher the rate of inflation.
    E. in the long run, the higher the rate of growth of the money supply, the higher the velocity of money.

19. The measure of the speed at which money circulates, or velocity, is equivalent to
    A. value of transactions divided by nominal GDP.
    B. nominal GDP times price divided by money supply.
    C. price times money supply divided by nominal GDP.
    D. nominal GDP divided by money supply.
    E. total value of transactions divided by nominal GDP.

20. The quantity equation
    A. states that the velocity of money is equal to the money supply times nominal GDP.
    B. implies that if velocity and real output are constant, an increase in inflation will cause an equal increase in the money supply in the long run.

C. implies that if velocity and real output are constant, an increase in the money supply will cause an equal increase in inflation in the long run.

D. implies that if velocity and real output are constant, an increase in the money supply will cause an equal increase in inflation in the short run.

E. implies that if velocity and real output are constant, an increase in inflation will cause an equal increase in the money supply in the short run.

Short Answer Problems
(Answers and solutions are given at the end of the chapter.)

1. Measuring the Money Supply

In this problem you will practice calculating the measures of the U.S. money supply—Ml and M2.

Month-Year	Currency	Savings deposits	Demand and other Checkable deposits	Money market mutual funds	Small time deposits
Aug-02	$616.3	$2,611.1	$562.1	$4,476.5	$909.0
Sep-02	616.1	2655.0	566.4	4498.7	901.1
Oct-02	617.0	2689.8	575.5	4526.6	894.3
Nov-02	622.8	2756.3	579.0	4589.7	888.2

Source: Federal Reserve Board of Governors Statistical Release January 3, 2003. All figures are in billions of dollars.

A. Use the preceding data to complete the following table, calculating the amounts for Ml and M2 for January through April 2000.

Month/Year	M1	M2
Aug-02		
Sep-02		
Oct-02		
Nov-02		

B. (b) If the public transfers funds from their (small) savings accounts at the Township Savings and Loan Association to their checking accounts at the Village Bank, this will (increase/decrease/leave unchanged)_____ M1, and (increase/decrease/leave unchanged)_____ M2.

C. (c) If the public deposits currency into their checking accounts at Village Bank, this will (increase/decrease/leave unchanged) _____ Ml, and (increase/decrease/leave unchanged) _____ M2.

2. Reserve/Deposit Ratio, Open-Market Operations, and Money Creation

In this problem you will calculate reserve/deposit ratios, determine how much a bank can lend based on its reserves, deposit liabilities and reserve/deposit ratio, and determine the effect of open-market sales and purchases of government securities on a bank's ability to lend and create money. Each question refers to the balance sheet of The Bank of Haute Finance shown below (i.e., do <u>not</u> take into account the transaction indicated in Questions 2A and 2C when answering Questions 2B and 2D).

Balance Sheet of
The Bank of Haute Finance

Assets	Liabilities
Currency (= reserves) $10,000	Deposits $10,000

A. If The Bank of Haute Finance has a desired reserve/deposit ratio of 10%, it can make new loans of $_____ in the form of new _____. After making the new loans The Bank of Haute Finance will have total deposit liabilities of $_____ , currency (= reserves) of $_____ , and outstanding loans of $_____ . Its total assets will then equal $_____ and its total liabilities will equal $_____ .

B. If the Fed imposes a minimum reserve/deposit ratio in the form of a 20% reserve requirement, the maximum amount of new loans The Bank of Haute Finance could make would be $_____ . After making the new loans The Bank of Haute Finance would have total deposit liabilities of $_____ , currency (= reserves) of $_____, and outstanding loans of $_____ . Its total assets would then equal $_____ and its total liabilities would equal $_____ .

C. Assume the Federal Reserve System buys $3000 of government securities from Susan Slavin and she deposits the $3000 in her checking account at The Bank of Haute Finance. Following the deposit, The Bank of Haute Finance would have currency (= reserves) of $_____ and deposit liabilities of $_____ . Assuming the Fed maintains a minimum reserve/deposit ratio of 20%, The Bank of Haute Finance could make new loans of $_____ . By doing so it would (increase/decrease) _____ the money supply by $_____ .

D. Assume the Federal Reserve System sells $3000 of government securities to The Bank of Haute Finance which it pays for out of its reserves. After the sale of the government securities, The Bank of Haute Finance would have currency (= reserves) of $_____ and deposit liabilities of $_____ . Assuming the Fed maintains a minimum reserve/deposit ratio of 20%, The Bank of Haute Finance could make new loans of $_____ . By doing so it would (increase/decrease) _____ the money supply by $_____ .

E. In comparing the answers to Questions 2B and 2D, by selling $3,000 of government securities to The Bank of Haute Finance, the Fed would be able to reduce the growth in the supply of money by $_____ .

3. Quantity Equation
This problem focuses on the relationship between the rate of growth of the money supply and inflation rates. You will practice calculating velocity and analyzing the relationship between growth in the money supply and inflation rates.

A. Complete the table below by calculating the velocity of M1 and M2 for

Date	M1	M2	Nominal GDP	Velocity of M1	Velocity of M2
Dec. 2001	$1,179.3	$5,458.6	$10,152.9		
Mar. 2002	$1,187.8	$5,493.0	$10,313.1		
June 2002	$1,190.2	$5,576.4	$10,376.9		
Sep. 2002	$1,191.2	$5,705.4	$10,506.2		

Sources: M1 and M2 data are from the Federal Reserve Board of Governors Statistical Release January 3, 2003, and Nominal GDP data are from the Bureau of Economic Analysis News Release, December 20, 2002. All figures are in billions of dollars.

B. Does the data below on the U.S. inflation rate and M1 growth rate support the conclusion that an increase in the supply of money will cause an exact increase in the inflation rate in the long run. _____
C. Does the data below support the weaker conclusion that higher rates of growth in the money supply will cause higher inflation rates?_____

_____

Dates	M1 Growth Rate	Inflation Rate
1961-70	51.9	33.6
1971-80	89.4	116.8
1981-90	100.6	53.8
1991-00	56.5	40.2

Source: The data were calculated from the Federal Reserve Economic Data (FRED II) available through the Federal Reserve Bank of St. Louis web site at http://research.stlouisfed.org/fred2/

IV. Economic Naturalist Application

In Economic Naturalist 10.1, it is explained that privately issued monies, such as Ithaca Hours and LETS (local electronic trading system), are alternative media of exchange in some communities where the law allows. The common characteristic of Ithaca Hours and LETS is that they function as a medium of exchange and, thus, facilitate trade. Credit cards are also issued by privately owned companies, typically banks, and are used to facilitate the purchase of goods and services. Discuss whether credit cards are privately issued monies.

V. Go to the Web: Graphing Exercises Using Interactive Graphs

How Can the Fed Offset Consumer Behavior?

> When consumers withdraw funds from their bank accounts and hold them as currency (out of fear that banks will go bankrupt and they will lose their money), the money supply and the economy are negatively affected. What actions can the Federal Reserve take to offset these changes in consumer behavior and keep the money supply and the economy at its desired level?
>
> Answer:

To review an answer to this question, and to learn more about the use of economic theory to analyze this issue (and other macroeconomic issues), please go to the Electronic Learning Session in the Student Center at the Frank/Bernanke web site: http://www.mhhe.com/economics/frankbernanke2.

VI. Self-Test Solutions

Key Terms
1. w
2. n
3. u
4. k
5. o
6. a
7. m
8. v
9. l
10. c
11. d
12. j
13. h
14. i
15. p
16. g
17. e
18. r
19. x
20. t
21. s
22. b

23. q
24. f

Multiple-Choice Questions

1. A
2. C
3. C
4. B
5. D
6. A
7. B With $50 million in reserves and $100 million in deposits, its reserve/deposit ratio of 1/2 is greater than its desired ratio. It would, therefore, increase its deposits to $150 million by making new loans.
8. E $10 million in new reserves divided by $40 million in new deposits equals .25 (the reserve/deposit ratio)
9. D
10. C
11. B
12. A
13. C
14. A
15. C
16. C
17. E Because each dollar of bank reserves translates into several dollars of money supply, the decrease in bank reserves is equal to the increase in currency that caused the money supply to decrease.
18. B
19. D
20. C

Short Answer Problems

1.
A.

Month/Year	M1	M2
Aug-02	$1,178.4	$9,175.0
Sep-02	$1,182.5	$9,237.3
Oct-02	$1,192.5	$9,303.2
Nov-02	$1,201.8	$9,436.0

B. increase; leave unchanged (because the components of M1 are also included in M2)
C. leave unchanged; leave unchanged (currency and checking deposits are included in both M1 and M2. Thus, depositing currency into a checking account does not change the amount of M1 or M2.)

2.

A. $90,000 (Because the desired reserve/deposit ratio is .10 the $10,000 in reserves can support $10,000/.10 = $100,000 in deposits. Thus, $100,000 minus the existing $10,000 in deposits = $90,000); checking deposits; $100,000; $10,000; $90,000; $100,000; $100,000

B. $40,000 (Now that the Fed has imposed a reserve requirements of .20, the $10,000 in reserves can support $10,000/.2 = $50,000. Thus, the bank can make new loan of $40,000); $50,000; $10,000; $40,000; $50,000; $50,000

C. $10,000 + $3,000 = $13,000; $13,000; $52,000 ($13,000/.2 = $65,000 from which the existing $13,000 is subtracted, allowing new loans of $52,000); increase; $52,000

D. $10,000 - $3,000 = $7,000; $7,000/.2 = $35,000 from which the existing $10,000 is subtracted, allowing new loans of $25,000; increase; $25,000 $50,000 - $25,000 = $25,000

3.

A.

Date	M1	M2	Nominal GDP	Velocity M1	Velocity M2
Dec. 2001	$1,179.3	$5,458.6	$10,152.9	8.61	1.86
Mar. 2002	$1,187.8	$5,493.0	$10,313.1	8.68	1.88
June 2002	$1,190.2	$5,576.4	$10,376.9	8.72	1.86
Sep. 2002	$1,191.2	$5,705.4	$10,506.2	8.82	1.84

B. No, the data does not support the extreme conclusion that an increase in the growth rate of money will lead to an exact increase in the inflation rate

C. With the exception of 1981-90, higher growth in M1 did lead to higher inflation in the U.S. Thus, the weaker conclusion that higher growth in the money supply will cause higher inflation is partially supported by the data.

Chapter 11
Financial Markets and
International Capital Flows

I. Pretest: What Do You Really Know?

Circle the letter that corresponds to the best answer. (Answers appear immediately after the final question).

1. Financial intermediaries are firms that
    A. extend credit to borrowers using funds from savers.
    B. match buyers and sellers of stocks.
    C. match buyers and sellers of bonds.
    D. conduct open-market operations.
    E. issue currency in exchange for government debt.

2. A legal promise to repay a debt is called
    A. equity.
    B. a stock.
    C. a bond.
    D. a dividend.
    E. the principal amount.

3. Stockholders receive returns on their financial investment in the form of _____ and _____.
    A. interest payments; dividends
    B. interest payments; deposits
    C. coupon payments; capital gains
    D. capital gains; interest payments
    E. capital gains; dividends

4. To the individual investor, a major advantage of mutual funds is
    A. increased interest income.
    B. increased diversification.
    C. increased riskiness.
    D. decreased diversification.
    E. increased dividends.

5. If domestic saving is greater than domestic investment, then a country will have a _____ and _____ net capital inflows.
   A. trade deficit; negative
   B. trade deficit; positive
   C. trade balance; zero
   D. trade surplus; negative
   E. trade surplus; positive

6. Purchases of foreign assets by domestic firms or households is called
   A. an import.
   B. an export.
   C. a capital outflow.
   D. a capital inflow.
   E. protectionism.

7. When a U.S. exporter sells software to France and uses the proceeds to buy stock in a French company, U.S. exports _____ and there is a capital _____ to/from the United States.
   A. increase; outflow
   B. increase; inflow
   C. do not change; outflow
   D. decrease; outflow
   E. decrease; inflow

8. In an open economy, a decrease in capital inflows _____ the equilibrium domestic real interest rate and _____ the quantity of domestic investment.
   A. increases; increases
   B. increases; decreases
   C. decreases; does not change
   D. decreases; increases
   E. decreases; decreases

9. If the United States has a $500 billion net capital inflow, then there must be
   A. a trade surplus of $500 billion.
   B. a trade deficit of $500 billion.
   C. no trade surplus or trade deficit.
   D. a net capital outflow of $1,000 billion.
   E. a trade surplus of $1,000 billion.

10. At each value of the domestic interest rate, a decrease in the riskiness of domestic assets _____ capital inflows, _____ capital outflows, and _____ net capital inflows.
    A. increases; increases; increases
    B. increases; increases; decreases
    C. increases; decreases; increases
    D. decreases; decreases; decreases
    E. decreases; increases; decreases

Solutions and Feedback to Pretest

For each question you incorrectly answered, we strongly recommend taking the time to review the appropriate material before continuing. In the table below, the relevant textbook pages are listed for each question as well as the pertinent Learning Objective from the following Key Point Review.

Correct Answer	Textbook Page Numbers	Learning Objective
1. A	p. 283	2
2. C	p. 285	3
3. E	pp. 287 - 89	4
4. B	pp. 290 - 91	5
5. D	pp. 292 - 94	6, 7
6. C	p. 292	7
7. A	pp. 292 - 94	7
8. B	pp. 295 - 97	7
9. E	pp. 298 - 99	7
10. B	pp. 294 -95	8

II. Key Point Review

The major financial markets and institutions and their role in directing saving to productive use are discussed in the first part of this chapter. In the second part, the international dimensions of capital and saving are discussed.

Learning Objective 1: Explain how market-oriented financial systems improve the allocation of saving.

A successful economy not only saves but also uses its saving to invest in projects that are most likely to be productive. In a market economy like that of the United States, savings are allocated by means of a decentralized, market-oriented financial system. A market-oriented financial system improves the allocation of savings by providing savers with information about the uses of their funds that are most likely to prove productive, and by helping savers share the risks of individual investment projects. Three key components of a market-oriented financial system are discussed in this chapter: (1) the banking systems, (2) the bond market, and (3) the stock market.

Learning Objective 2: Define financial intermediaries and explain the role of financial intermediaries in a market economy.

Financial intermediaries are firms that extend credit to borrowers using funds raised from savers. The most important financial intermediaries in the banking system are the commercial banks. They are privately owned firms that accept deposits from individuals and businesses and use those deposits to make loans. Savers are willing to hold bank deposits because banks (and other financial intermediaries) have a comparative advantage in information-gathering about lending opportunities that results in lower costs and better results than individual savers could achieve on their own. Banks also make it easier for households and business to make payments for goods and services.

Note: Banks and other financial intermediaries have gained experience in evaluating potential borrowers and monitoring borrowers' activities. This not only benefits the banks and savers, but also helps the borrowers by providing access to credit that may otherwise not be available.

Learning Objective 3: Explain how bond markets can be a source of funds for businesses; define bond, principal amount, coupon rate and coupon payment.

In addition to obtaining funds from banks, corporations and governments can obtain funds in the bond market. Corporations and governments frequently raise funds by issuing bonds and selling them to savers. A **bond** is a legal promise to repay a debt, usually including both the **principal amount** (the amount originally lent) and regular interest payments. The promised interest rate when a bond is issued is called the **coupon rate**, which is paid to the bondholder in regular interest payments called **coupon payments**. The coupon rate must be sufficiently attractive to savers, depending upon the term, or length of time before the debt is fully repaid, and the risk that the borrower will not repay the debt. Bonds also differ in terms of their tax treatment. The interest on municipal bonds, issued by local governments, is exempt from federal income taxes and, thus, typically pays a lower coupon rate than do other comparable bonds. Bondholders do not have to hold bonds until they are to be repaid by the issuer because they can sell them in the bond market. The price (or market value) of a bond at any point in time is inversely related to interest rates being paid on comparable newly issued bonds.

Hint: Because bond prices and interest rates are inversely related, if interest rates on new bond issues rise, the price a bond holder will received for an outstanding bond will fall. That is, if you are holding a bond that pays an interest rate of six percent annually, and new bond issues are now paying seven percent annually, you will only be able to sell the bond to another investor if you price the bond sufficiently low to allow the investor to earn the seven percent rate of return that the investor could earn elsewhere. The price would be below what you paid for the bond and would result in a capital loss.

Learning Objective 4: Explain the role of the stock markets; define stock dividend and risk premium.

Another important way of raising funds, but one that is restricted to corporations, is by issuing stock to the public. A share of **stock**, also called equity, is a claim to partial ownership of a firm. Stockholders receive returns on their financial investment in a firm through dividend payments and capital gains (the increase in the price of the stock). A **dividend** is a regular payment received by stockholders for each share that they own, as determined by the firm's management, and is usually dependent on the firm's recent profits. The price of a share of stock at any point in time depends on the expected future dividends and capital gain, adjusted for the risk premium. **Risk premium** is the rate of return that financial investors require to hold risky assets minus the rate of return on safe assets.

Learning Objective 5: Define diversification and explain the role of mutual funds.
Like banks, bond and stock markets provide a means of channeling funds from savers to
borrowers with productive investment opportunities. Savers and their financial advisors search
for high returns in the bond and stock markets and, thus, provide a powerful incentive to
potential borrowers to use the funds productively. The markets also give savers a means to
diversify their financial investments. **Diversification** is the practice of spreading ones wealth
over a variety of financial investments in order to reduce overall risk. From society's perspective,
diversification makes it possible for risky but worthwhile projects to obtain funding without
individual savers having to bear too much risk. For the typical saver, a convenient way to
diversify is buy stocks and bonds indirectly through mutual funds. A **mutual fund** is a financial
intermediary that sells shares in itself to the public, then uses the funds raised to buy a wide
variety of financial assets.

> **Note**: In the past, small investors with limited funds to invest would
> find it very difficult to achieve a diversified portfolio of investments by
> directly purchasing individual stocks and bonds. Most small investors,
> therefore, did little more than put their saving into saving accounts. But
> in recent years with the rapid growth in the number of stock and bond
> mutual funds, small investors have increasingly been able to reduce the
> risks of investing and simultaneously increase their rate of return by
> purchasing shares of stock and bond mutual funds.

**Learning Objective 6: Define trade balance, trade surplus, and trade deficit and capital
flows.**
When an economy is open to trade, its **trade balance**, the value of a country's exports minus the
value of its imports in a particular period, may be positive or negative. A country is said to have
a **trade surplus** for a period when the value of its exports exceeds the value of its imports.
Alternatively, a country is said to have a **trade deficit** for a period when the value of its imports
exceeds the value of its exports. In addition to the trade of goods and services that is captured in
the trade balance, trade among countries occurs in real and financial assets.

**Learning Objective 7: Discuss the relationships among international capital flows and
domestic saving and investment.**
Purchases or sales of real and financial assets across international borders are known as
international capital flows. From the perspective of a particular country, purchases of domestic
assets by foreigners are called **capital inflows**, and purchases of foreign assets by domestic
households and firms are called **capital outflows**. Capital inflows are related to real interest rates
and investment risk in a country. The higher the real interest rate in a country, and the lower the
risk of investing there, the higher its capital inflows. Capital inflows expand a country's pool of
saving, allowing for more domestic investment and economic growth. A drawback, however, to
using capital inflows to finance domestic investment is that the interest and dividends on the
borrowed funds must be paid to foreign savers rather than domestic residents.

Learning Objective 8: Explain the link between the trade balance and capital flows.
There is a precise link between the trade balance and international capital flows. In any given
period, the trade balance and net capital inflows add up to zero, or NX (net exports) + KI (net

capital inflows) = 0. This link suggests the primary cause of a trade deficit is a country's low rate of national saving. A low-saving, high-spending country is likely to import more and export less than a high-saving, low-spending country. It is also likely to have higher real interest rates, attracting capital inflows. Because the sum of the trade balance and capital inflows is zero, a high level of net capital inflows is consistent with a large trade deficit.

Note: In theory, it is impossible for a country to continuously run a trade deficit because the capital inflows will eventually decrease the value of its currency vis-à-vis other currencies. As this happens, the cost of imports will increase and it will import less, and its exports will become more competitive and its exports will grow. As a result, net exports will rise and its trade deficit will decline.

III. Self-Test

Key Terms
Match the term in the right-hand column with the appropriate definitions in the left-hand column by placing the letter of the term in the blank in front of its definition. (Answers are given at the end of the chapter.)

1. _____ Firms that extend credit to borrowers using funds raised from savers.

    a. bond

2. _____ A regular payment received by stockholders for each share that they own.

    b. capital inflows

3. _____ The value of a country's exports less the value of its imports in a particular period (quarter or year).

    c. capital outflows

4. _____ When imports exceed exports, the difference between the value of a country's imports and the value of its exports in a given period.

    d. coupon payment

5. _____ A legal promise to repay a debt, usually including both the principal amount and regular interest payments.

    e. coupon rate

6. _____ The practice of spreading of ones wealth over a variety of different financial investments to reduce overall risk.

    f. diversification

7. _____ When exports exceed imports, the difference between the value of a country's exports and the value of its imports in a given period.

    g. dividend

8. _____ A financial intermediary that sells shares in itself to the public, then uses the funds raised to buy a wide variety of financial assets.

    h. financial intermediaries

9. _____ The amount originally lent.

    i. international capital flows

10. _____ A claim to partial ownership of a firm.

    j. mutual fund

11. _____ Purchases or sales of real and financial assets across international borders.

    k. principal amount

12. _____ The interest rate promised when a bond is issued.

    l. risk premium

13.____ Purchases of foreign assets by domestic households and   m. stock
firms.
14.____ The rate of return that financial investors require to hold   n. trade balance (or
risky assets minus the rate of return on safe assets.   net exports)
15.____Regular interest payments made to the bondholder.   o. trade deficit
16.____ Purchases of domestic assets by foreign households and   p. trade surplus
firms.

Multiple-Choice Questions
Circle the letter that corresponds to the best answer. (Answers are given at the end of the chapter.)

1. A market-oriented financial system improves the allocation of savings by providing
    A. information about savers and helping savers share the risks of individual investment projects.
    B. information to savers about the risks of individual investment projects and helping investors reduce the risks of individual investment projects.
    C. information to savers about alternative productive uses for funds and helping savers share the risks of individual investment projects.
    D. banks with a comparative advantage over small savers in evaluating and monitoring prospective borrowers.
    E. information to financial intermediaries and to stock and bond markets about alternative productive uses for funds and by reducing the risk to savers through diversification.

2. Banks and other financial intermediaries are necessary because they
    A. have a comparative advantage in evaluating the quality of borrowers.
    B. shift the risk of investing from borrowers to savers.
    C. facilitate the direct lending of funds by savers to borrowers.
    D. diversify the risk of saving.
    E. eliminate the need to gather information about borrowers.

3. A feature common to all financial intermediaries is that they
    A. buy and sell information about savers and borrowers.
    B. have a comparative advantage in gathering and evaluating information about borrowers.
    C. act as agents for buyers and sellers in the money market.
    D. shift the risk of investing from borrowers to savers.
    E. collect funds from a few savers and distribute the funds to many borrowers.

4. Which of the following sources of funds are available to large and well-established corporations but not to the typical small borrower?
    A. Financial intermediaries and bond markets
    B. Municipal bond and stock markets
    C. Financial intermediaries and stock and bond markets
    D. Stock and corporate bond markets
    E. There are no sources of funds available to large and well-established corporations that are not available to the small borrower.

5. In comparison to a corporate bond, a municipal bond of the same term and credit risk will have a
   A. higher risk premium.
   B. higher coupon payment.
   C. higher coupon rate.
   D. lower coupon rate.
   E. same coupon rate.

6. Since the early 1990s, the Japanese banking system has
   A. experienced severe financial problems that have contributed to the severe economic downturn in Japan.
   B. acquired corporate stocks and made loans to real estate developers that have contributed to an economic boom in Japan.
   C. experienced severe financial problems that created a "credit crunch" for large corporations in Japan.
   D. experienced severe financial problems that created a "credit crunch" for small- and medium-sized businesses worldwide.
   E. experienced severe financial problems that has forced the Japanese government to provide the banks with huge amounts of capital to return them to a healthy financial condition.

7. The price of a share of corporate stock varies over time depending upon stockholders' expectations about the future
   A. coupon rate, risk premium, and coupon payment.
   B. dividend, stock price, and coupon rate.
   C. coupon payment, dividend, and risk premium.
   D. coupon rate, coupon premium, and dividend.
   E. dividend, stock price, and risk premium

8. The informational role of the stock and bond markets provides incentives for savers and their financial advisors to
   A. direct funds to those borrowers that appear to have the safest investments.
   B. direct funds to those borrowers that appear to have the most productive investments.
   C. diversify their investments by purchasing mutual funds.
   D. shift the risk of investing to the borrowers.
   E. avoid the cost of paying the financial intermediaries by going directly to the borrowers to make loans.

9. Antonio holds a two-year bond issued by the Jetson Corporation with a principal amount of $10,000. The annual coupon rate is 6 percent. He considered selling it after receiving the first coupon payment a week ago at a price of $9,390. Since that time, the coupon rate on new bond issues has risen from to 7.0%. If he were to sell the bond today, the price would be
   A. $10,000.
   B. higher than it was a week ago.
   C. the same at it was a week ago.
   D. lower than it was a week ago.
   E. impossible to determine from the information given.

10. When American investors pay cash for stock in a French corporation, from the perspective of
    A. the United States, it is a capital inflow.
    B. France, it is a capital outflow.
    C. the United States, it is a capital outflow.
    D. France, it is a trade deficit.
    E. the United States, it is a trade deficit.

11. If interest rates in Japan increase relative to international interest rate levels, all else being equal, Japan's net capital
    A. inflows will tend to increase, and the pool of funds for domestic investment will tend to decrease.
    B. inflows will tend to increase, and the pool of funds for domestic investment will tend to increase.
    C. outflows will tend to increase, and the pool of funds for domestic investment will tend to decrease.
    D. outflows will tend to increase, and the pool of funds for domestic investment will tend to increase.
    E. inflows will tend to decrease, and the pool of funds for domestic investment will tend to decrease.

12. The sum of national saving and capital inflows from abroad must equal
    A. domestic investment in new capital goods.
    B. capital outflows.
    C. aggregate demand.
    D. the trade deficit.
    E. the trade surplus.

13. The U.S. trade deficit is mainly caused by
    A. production of inferior goods in the country.
    B. unfair trade restrictions imposed by other countries on imports.
    C. a low rate of national saving.
    D. cheap labor in other countries.
    E. inadequate safety and environmental protections in other countries.

14. Which of the following transactions would cause a capital inflow to a country?
    A. exports of goods or services
    B. import of goods or services
    C. purchasing financial assets (e.g., a corporate bond) from abroad
    D. purchasing real assets (e.g., a factory) abroad
    E. lending money abroad

15. The illegal drug trade has increased the political instability in Colombia and has
    A. reduced net capital outflows from Colombia.
    B. reduced net capital inflows to Colombia.
    C. increased net capital inflows to Colombia.
    D. increased Colombia's trade deficit.

E. decreased Colombia's trade surplus.

16. An increase in net capital inflows to a country will
    A. increase its real interest rates.
    B. increase its imports.
    C. decrease its exports.
    D. decrease its real interest rates.
    E. decrease its investment in new capital.

17. During the 1960s and 1970s, the U.S. trade balance was close to zero, but during the 1980s the trade deficit ballooned to unprecedented levels due to
    A. an inability of U.S. companies to compete in the international market.
    B. a decline in private saving that resulted from an upsurge in consumption.
    C. a decline in national saving without a corresponding decrease in investment.
    D.   a worldwide recession that made it difficult for U. S. companies to sell their products abroad.
    E. unfair protectionist policies imposed by major trading partners of the U.S.

18. A country's trade balance and its net capital inflows
    A. add up to zero.
    B. determine the size of the pool of saving available for capital investment.
    C. must always equal the sum of the four components of aggregate demand.
    D. must equal domestic investment in new capital goods.
    E. are identical in open and closed economies.

19. Capital inflows used to finance capital investment in some developing countries have
    A. decreased domestic saving.
    B. benefited domestic savers because of higher interest rates paid on saving accounts.
    C. caused debt crises because the returns on the investments were less than the interest cost of the capital.
    D. caused debt crises because the returns on the investments were greater than the interest cost of the capital.
    E. had economic benefits without costs.

20. The Argentine economic collapse in 2001-02 was caused by
    A. an increase in domestic savings rates and a corresponding decline in domestic consumption spending that led to a collapse in production.
    B. an insufficient level of skilled and educated workers in the growing high tech industries.
    C. the International Monetary Fund's refusal to provide additional loans to the Argentine government to pay its foreign debt.
    D. Argentina defaulting on its foreign debt and the subsequent unwillingness of foreign lenders to make additional loans.
    E. Argentina defaulting on its foreign debt because the Argentine government's spending exceeded its tax revenues.

Short Answer Problems
(Answers and solutions are given at the end of the chapter.)

1. Bond and Stock Prices
This problem will require you to calculate the effects of various factors on the price of bonds and stocks.

A. Carley has purchased a newly issued bond from the SimonSays Corp. for $10,000. The SimonSays Corp. will pay the bondholder $750 at the end of years 1-4 and will pay $10,750 at the end of year 5. The bond has a principal amount of $_____, a term of _____ years, a coupon rate of _____ %, and a coupon payment of $_____ .

B. After receiving coupon payments 1 through 4, Carley has decided to sell the bond. What price should she expect to receive if the one-year interest rate on comparable financial assets is 5%? $_____ What price should she expect to receive if the one-year interest rate on comparable financial assets is 8%? $_____

C. Justin has decided to buy 100 shares of stock in The Boot Company. He expects the company to pay a dividend of $3 per share in one year and expects the price of the shares will be $40 at that time. How much should he be willing to pay today per share if the safe rate of interest is 7% and The Boot Company carries no risk? $_____

D. How much should Justin be willing to pay today per share if the safe rate of interest is 5% and The Boot Company carries no risk? $_____

E. How much should Justin be willing to pay today per share if the safe rate of interest is 5% and he requires a risk premium of 2%? $_____

2. International Capital Flows
This problem focuses on the determinants of international capital flows, including risks and domestic and international interest rates.

A. The graph below shows the net capital inflows to the United States for 2003. What level of domestic interest rate is necessary for net capital inflows to be positive? _____ percent

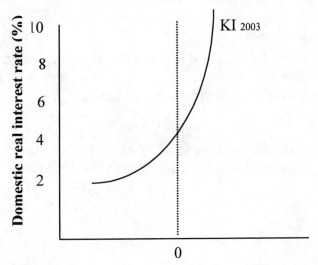

B. On the graph above, sho **Net capital inflows *KI*** iskiness of domestic assets (label the new curve KI₁).

C. On the graph above, show the impact of an increase in real interest rates abroad (label the new curve KI2).

D. On the graph above, show the impact of an increase in riskiness of assets abroad (label the new curve KI3).

3. Saving, Investment and Capital Flows in an Open Economy
This problem expands upon the saving-investment diagram for a closed economy by focusing on the effects of international capital flows on domestic interest rates and investment.

A. In an open economy the amount of investment must be equal to _____ plus
_____ .

B. The graph below shows domestic saving (S) and domestic investment (I) curves. Draw a new curve that would show the impact of opening the domestic financial markets to capital inflows (label the new curve S + KI).

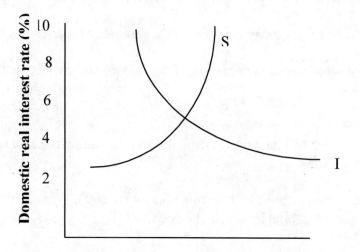

Saving and Investment

C. As a result of opening the domestic economy to capital inflows, the domestic equilibrium interest rate will (decrease/increase/remain unchanged) _____ and the equilibrium level of saving and investment will (decrease/increase/remain unchanged)
_____ .

D. As the economy is opened, if capital inflows allow the level of investment to exceed the amount of national saving, then the country must also have a trade (surplus/deficit)
_____ .

IV. Economic Naturalist Application

In Economic Naturalist 11.4, the relationship between the U.S. trade deficit and the
level of national saving and investment is explained. It is noted that the large U.S.
trade deficits during the mid-1980s and the latter part of the 1990s correspond to
periods in which investment in the U.S. exceeded national saving. Starting in early
2001, capital investment spending has plummeted in the U.S. as the high tech
"bubble" has burst. Discuss the implications of the collapse in U.S. investment
spending on the U.S. trade deficit. Note: explicitly state your assumptions about the
future level of national saving.

V. Go to the Web: Graphing Exercises Using Interactive Graphs

What is the Relationship between the U.S. Federal Budget Deficit and the U.S. Trade Deficit?

Both the U.S. federal budget deficit and the U.S. trade deficit ballooned during the
1980s, leading some economists to label them the "twin deficits" because of their
seemingly related behavior. However, during the 1990s, the federal budget deficit
shrank and eventually turned to a surplus, while the U.S. trade deficit increased to
record levels. How can the open-economy saving-investment model developed in this
chapter explain this behavior?
Answer:

To review an answer to this question, and to learn more about the use of economic theory to
analyze this issue (and other macroeconomic issues), please go to the Electronic Learning
Session in the Student Center at the Frank/Bernanke web site:
http://www.mhhe.com/economics/frankbernanke2.

VI. Self-Test Solutions

Key Terms
1. h
2. g
3. n
4. o
5. a
6. f
7. p
8. j
9. k

10. m
11. i
12. e
13. c
14. l
15. d
16. b

Multiple-Choice Questions

1. C
2. A
3. B
4. D
5. D Because municipal bonds are exempt from federal income taxes, they have a lower coupon rate than comparable nonmunicipal bonds.
6. A
7. E
8. B
9. D
10. C
11. B
12. A
13. C
14. A
15. B
16. D
17. C
18. A
19. C
20. D

Short Answer Problems

1.
A. $10,000; 5; 7.5%; $750
B. $10,750 / 1.05 = $10, 238.10; $9,953.70
C. $43 / 1.07 = $40.95
D. $43 / 1.05 = $40.19
E. $43 / (1.05 + .02) = $40.19

2.

A. 4

B.

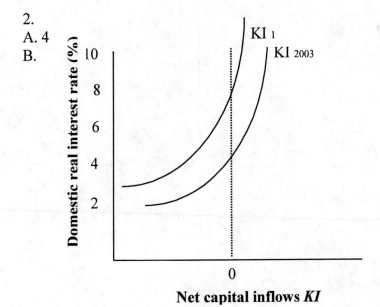

C.

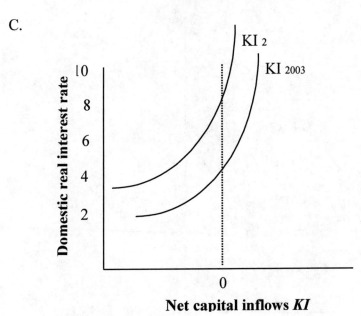

D.

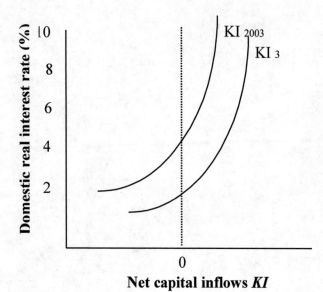

3.
A. saving; capital inflows
B.

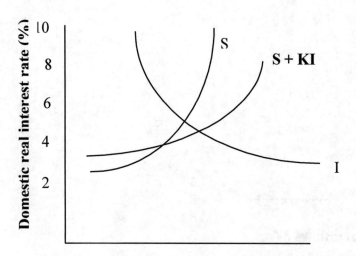

C. decrease; increase
D. deficit

Chapter 12
Short-term Economic Fluctuations:
An Introduction

I. Pretest: What Do You Really Know?

Circle the letter that corresponds to the best answer. (Answers appear immediately after the final question).

1. Since the end of World War II, recessions in the U.S have _____ than expansions.
   A. occurred more frequently
   B. been shorter in duration, on average,
   C. been longer in duration, on average,
   D. generated more inflation
   E. been more predictable

2. Economic activity moves from a trough into a period of _____ until it reaches a _____ and then into a period of _____.
   A. expansion; trough; recession.
   B. recession; trough; expansion
   C. expansion; peak; recession
   D. recession; peak; expansion
   E. expansion; trough; expansion

3. In reference to short-term economic fluctuations, the "peak" refers to
   A. a period in which the economy is growing at a rate significantly above normal.
   B. the high point of economic activity prior to a downturn.
   C. the low point of economic activity prior to a recovery.
   D. a particularly strong and protracted expansion.
   E. a particularly severe and protracted recession.

4. An expansion is
   A. a period in which the economy is growing at a rate significantly below normal.
   B. a period in which the economy is growing at a rate significantly above normal.
   C. the high point of economic activity prior to a downturn.
   D. the low point of economic activity prior to a recovery.
   E. a particularly severe or protracted recession.

5. The following data give the dates of successive turning points in U.S. economic activity and the corresponding levels of real GDP at the time:

Turning Point	Date	Real GDP(1996 $ billions)
(A)	Jan. 1980	4958.9
(B)	July 1980	4850.3
(C)	July 1981	5056.8
(D)	Nov. 1982	4912.1
(E)	July 1990	6731.7

   Which of the following periods is a recession?
   A. Jan. 1980 through July 1980
   B. Jan. 1980 through July 1981
   C. July 1980 through July 1981
   D. July 1980 though Nov. 1982
   E. Nov. 1982 through July 1990

6. All of the following are characteristics of short-term economic fluctuations *except*
   A. expansions and recessions are felt throughout the economy.
   B. expansions and recessions are irregular in length and severity.
   C. unemployment falls sharply during recessions.
   D. durable goods industries are more sensitive to short-term fluctuations than are service and nondurable goods industries.
   E. recessions tend to be followed by a decline in inflation.

7. Which of the following workers is most likely to lose his/her job during a recession?
   A. construction worker
   B. baker
   C. farmer
   D. barber
   E. police officer

8. The difference between the economy's potential output and its actual output at a point in time is called the
   A. budget deficit.
   B. trade deficit.
   C. output gap.
   D. full-employment rate.
   E. cyclical peak.

9. If potential output equals $5 billion and actual output equals $3.5 billion, then this economy has a(n)
   A. budget deficit.
   B. trade deficit.
   C. expansionary gap.
   D. recessionary gap.
   E. value-added gap.

10. In Macroland potential GDP equals $8 trillion and real GDP equals $7.6 trillion. Macroland has a(n) _____ gap equal to _____ percent of potential GDP.
    A. expansionary; -5
    B. expansionary; 5
    C. recessionary; -5
    D. recessionary; 5
    E. recessionary; 6

Solutions and Feedback to Pretest

For each question you incorrectly answered, we strongly recommend taking the time to review the appropriate material before continuing. In the table below, the relevant textbook pages are listed for each question as well as the pertinent Learning Objective from the following Key Point Review.

Correct Answer	Textbook Page Numbers	Learning Objective
1. B	pp. 309 - 11	1
2. C	pp. 309 - 11	1
3. B	pp. 309 - 11	1
4. B	pp. 309 - 11	1
5. A	pp. 309 - 11	1
6. C	pp. 312 - 14	2
7. A	pp. 312 - 14	2
8. C	pp. 315 - 16	3
9. D	pp. 315 - 16	3
10. D	pp. 315 - 16	3

II. Key Point Review

In the preceding section of the book, the factors that determine long-run economic growth and living standards were discussed. While long-run economic conditions are the ultimate determinant of living standards, short-run fluctuations in economic conditions are also important. The history, characteristics, and causes of the short-run fluctuations in economic conditions are discussed in this chapter. The chapter concludes with a preview of the causes of recessions and expansions, which are discussed in greater detail in the next three chapters.

Learning Objective 1: Define recession, depression, expansion, boom, peak, and trough.
The short-run fluctuations in economic conditions are commonly known as recessions and expansions. A **recession**, or contraction, is a period in which the economy is growing at a rate

significantly below normal. An extremely severe or protracted recession is called a **depression**. A more informal definition of a recession (often used by the mass media) is a period during which real GDP falls for at least two consecutive quarters. While the "two consecutive quarters" rule would not classify a slow-growth episode as a recession, many economists would argue that a period in which real GDP growth is significantly below normal should be counted as a recession. The beginning of a recession is called a **peak**, the high point of economic activity prior to a downturn. The end of a recession, marking the low point of economic activity prior to a recovery, is called a **trough**. By far the longest and most severe recession in the United States was during 1929-33. Since World War II, U.S. recessions have generally been short, lasting between six and sixteen months. The opposite of a recession is an **expansion**, a period in which the economy is growing at a rate that is significantly above normal. A particularly strong and protracted expansion is called a **boom**. On average, expansions have lasted longer than recessions. The two longest expansions were during 1961-69, and the one following the trough of 1990-91 (in February, 2000 this boom broke the all-time record for the duration of a U.S. expansion).

Learning Objective 2: Discuss the characteristics of short-term economic fluctuations.
Expansions and recessions are not new, as they have been a feature of industrial economies since at least the late 18th century. Short-run economic fluctuations, although they are sometimes referred to as business cycles, or cyclical fluctuations, do not recur at predictable intervals but are quite irregular in their length and severity. This irregularity makes it extremely hard to predict the dates of peaks and troughs. Expansions and recessions are felt throughout the national economy, and even globally. Unemployment is a key indicator of short-term fluctuations, typically rising during recessions and falling (although more slowly) during expansions. Cyclical unemployment is the type of unemployment associated with recessions. In addition to rising unemployment, labor market conditions become more unfavorable during recessions, with real wages growing more slowly and workers less likely to receive promotions or bonuses. Inflation also follows a typical pattern during recessions and expansions, though not as sharply defined. Recessions tend to be preceded by increases in inflation and followed soon after by a decline in inflation. Durable goods industries tend to be more affected by recessions and expansions, while services and nondurable goods industries are less sensitive to short-term economic fluctuations.

Learning Objective 3: Define potential output, output gap, recessionary gap, and expansionary gap.
Economists measure expansions and recessions by determining how far output is from its normal level. The normal level of output is called **potential output** (also known as potential GDP or full-employment output): the amount of output (real GDP) that an economy can produce when using its resources, such as capital and labor, at normal rates. Actual output (real GDP) may be below or above potential output at any point in time. The difference between potential output and actual output is called the **output gap**. The output gap is expressed in symbols as $Y^* - Y$. A positive output gap, when actual output is below potential output and resources are not fully utilized, is called a **recessionary gap**. A negative output gap, when actual output is above potential output and resources are utilized at above-normal rates, is called an **expansionary gap**.

Note: Be careful to not become confused by the terminology regarding output gaps. Sometimes students mistakenly think that because actual output is below potential, the output gap should be negative. When actual output is below potential output there is a **positive** output gap. When actual output is above potential output there is a **negative** output gap.

Learning Objective 4: Define the natural rate of unemployment and explain its relationship to cyclical unemployment.

Recessionary gaps are associated with below-normal utilization of labor resources. This is another way of saying there is "extra" unemployment during recessions. Specifically, in addition to the frictional and structural unemployment, which are always present in the labor market, cyclical unemployment is present during recessions. Economists call that part of the total unemployment rate that is attributable to frictional and structural unemployment the **natural rate of unemployment**. The natural rate of unemployment can vary over time because of changes in frictional and/or structural unemployment. The natural rate of unemployment is the unemployment rate that prevails when cyclical unemployment is zero. Cyclical unemployment can, therefore, be calculated as the difference between the actual unemployment rate (u) and the natural rate of unemployment (u^*). During recessions cyclical unemployment is positive and during expansions it is negative.

Hint: The concept of a "natural" rate of unemployment is intended to reflect the fact that there is always some amount of unemployment in the economy, i.e., it is a natural state of the economy. Thus, it is virtually impossible for the unemployment rate to ever equal zero.

Learning Objective 5: Define Okun's Law and explain its importance to understanding short-run fluctuations in the economy.

The relationship between the output gap and the amount of cyclical unemployment is given by Okun's Law. **Okun's Law** states that each extra percentage point of cyclical unemployment is associated with about a two-percentage point increase in the output gap. The output losses calculated according to Okun's Law suggest that recessions have significant costs (which are reflected, for example, in the importance that short-run economic fluctuations have on presidential elections in the United States).

Note: Be careful to not mistakenly interpret Okun's Law to indicate that the change in unemployment *causes* the output gap. The cause-and-effect works in the opposite direction. That is, an increase in output gap causes unemployment to rise. It is, however, much easier to observe changes in unemployment that changes in output gaps. Thus, Okun's Law is more of a rule of thumb than an analytical theory.

Learning Objective 6: Explain why short-run fluctuations occur.
In the short run, prices do not always adjust immediately to changing demand or supply as some producers vary the quantity of output rather than price, meeting the demand at a preset price. In the short run, therefore, changes in economy-wide spending are the primary cause of output gaps. In the long run, however, prices will adjust to their market-clearing levels, as producers better understand the information provided by the market, and output will equal potential output. The quantities of inputs, and the productivity with which they are used, are the primary determinants of economic activity in the long run. While total spending in the economy affects output in the short run, in the long run its main effects are on prices.

III. Self-Test

Key Terms
Match the term in the right-hand column with the appropriate definitions in the left-hand column by placing the letter of the term in the blank in front of its definition. (Answers are given at the end of the chapter.)

1. ____A particularly strong and protracted expansion.
2. ____ The amount of output (real GDP) that an economy can produce when using its resources, such as capital and labor, at normal rates.
3. ____ Each extra percentage point of cyclical unemployment is associated with about a 2 percentage point increase in the output gap, measured in relation to potential output.
4. ____ An extremely severe or protracted recession.
5. ____ A negative output gap, which occurs when actual output is above potential output
6. ____ The end of a recession, the low point of economic activity prior to a recovery.
7. ____The difference between the economy's potential output and its actual output at some point in time.
8. ____ A period in which the economy is growing at a rate significantly below normal.
9. ____ The part of the total unemployment rate that is attributable to frictional and structural unemployment.
10.____ The beginning or a recession, the high point of economic activity prior to a downturn.
11.____ A period in which the economy is growing at a rate that is significantly above normal.
12.____ A positive output gap, which occurs when potential output exceeds actual output.

a. boom
b. depression
c. expansion
d. expansionary gap
e. natural rate of unemployment
f. Okun's Law
g. output gap
h. peak
i. potential output
j. recession
k. recessionary gap
l. trough

Multiple-Choice Questions
Circle the letter that corresponds to the best answer. (Answers are given at the end of the chapter.)

1. The longest and most severe recession in the United States was during
    A. August 1957 to February 1961, initiating what became known as the Great Depression.
    B. November 1973 to March 1975, initiating what became known as the Great Depression.
    C. May 1937 to June 1938, initiating what became known as the Great Depression.
    D. January 1980 to November 1982, initiating what became known as the Great Depression.
    E. August 1929 to March 1933, initiating what became known as the Great Depression.

2. Short-term economic fluctuations
    A. recur at predictable intervals.
    B. have a limited impact on a few industries or regions.
    C. contain peaks and troughs that are easily predicted by professional forecasters.
    D. are irregular in their length and severity.
    E. have little impact on unemployment and inflation.

3. Unemployment typically
    A. is unaffected by recessions and expansions.
    B. rises during recession and falls during expansions.
    C. falls during recessions and rises during expansions.
    D. rises during recessions and falls during expansions, as does inflation.
    E. falls during recessions and rises during expansions, as does inflation.

4. The Japanese economy slowed markedly during the 1990s due to
    A. faster growth in potential output combined with a significant output gap.
    B. slower growth in potential output, and actual output equal to potential output.
    C. slower growth in potential output combined with a significant output gap.
    D. faster growth in potential output, and actual output equal to potential output.
    E. normal growth in potential output combined with a significant output gap.

5. As the average age of U.S. workers has increased since 1980
    A. frictional unemployment has fallen and the natural rate of unemployment has decreased.
    B. cyclical unemployment has fallen and the natural rate of unemployment has decreased.
    C. structural unemployment has fallen and the natural rate of unemployment has decreased.
    D. frictional unemployment has risen and the natural rate of unemployment has increased.
    E. cyclical unemployment has risen and the natural rate of unemployment has increased.

6. If cyclical unemployment rises to 2.5% and potential output (GDP) equals $9,000 billion, the output gap would equal
    A. $22,500 billion.
    B. $225 billion.
    C. $9,000 billion.
    D. $8,775 billion.
    E. $9,225 billion.

7. The firm behavior known as "meeting the demand " refers to
    A. firms adjusting prices from moment to moment in response to changes in demand.
    B. firms adjusting prices continuously in order to ensure that the quantity supplied equals the quantity demanded.
    C. changes in economy-wide spending as the primary cause of output gaps.
    D. price changes that eliminate output gaps in a self-correcting market.
    E. firms adjusting prices only periodically, while in the short run varying the quantity of output.

8. A recessionary gap occurs when
    A. total spending is abnormally high.
    B. total spending is at normal levels, but potential output is growing at abnormally high levels.
    C. total spending is low for some reason.
    D. potential output is less than actual output.
    E. actual output is greater than potential output.

9. The self-correcting market mechanism eliminates output gaps over time through price
    A. decreases if demand exceeds potential output.
    B. increases if demand is less than potential output.
    C. decreases if an expansionary gap exists.
    D. decreases if a recessionary gap exists.
    E. increases if a recessionary gap exists.

10. The longest expansion in the U.S. economy
    A. began in August 1929, at the trough of the Great Depression.
    B. lasted 106 months.
    C. began in March 1991, at the trough of the 1990-91 recession.
    D. lasted 92 months.
    E. began in February 1961, at the trough of the 1960-61 recession.

11. On average, recessions in the United States have been
    A. shorter than expansions.
    B. longer than expansions.
    C. longer and more severe during the post-WWII period than prior to WWII.
    D. shorter but more severe during the post-WWII period than prior to WWII.
    E. equal in duration to expansions.

12. During short-term economic fluctuations, inflation tends to
    A. rise following an economic peak and fall soon after the trough.
    B. fall following an economic peak and rise soon after the trough.
    C. rise following an economic peak and rise soon after the trough.
    D. fall following an economic peak and rise soon after the trough.
    E. move in the same direction as unemployment.

13. An economy grows significantly below its normal rate when
    A. actual output is above potential output.
    B. actual output equals potential output, but potential output is growing very slowly.
    C. actual output equals potential output, but potential output is growing very rapidly.
    D. actual output is below potential output and potential output is growing very rapidly.
    E. actual output is above potential output and potential output is growing very rapidly.

14. An expansionary gap implies that resources are
    A. not being fully utilized and the unemployment rate would be above the natural rate of unemployment.
    B. being utilized at above-normal rates and the unemployment rate would be above the natural rate of unemployment.
    C. not being fully utilized and the unemployment rate would be below the natural rate of unemployment.
    D. being utilized at above-normal rates and cyclical unemployment is positive.
    E. being utilized at above-normal rates and cyclical unemployment is negative.

15. In some markets, such as the market for grain, price-setting by auction occurs, but in other markets it does not because
    A. there are not enough auctioneers to announce prices for all the markets.
    B. auctions are inefficient when there are a small number of customers and low sales volume at any given time.
    C. auctions are inefficient when a market has a large number of buyers and sellers and a large volume of standardized goods.
    D. auctions are not feasible when the goods are perishable (e.g., ice cream).
    E. the economic benefits of auctions are less than the economic costs of auctions in markets for perishable goods.

16. In the long run
    A. prices adjust to market-clearing levels, and output equals potential output.
    B. prices adjust to market-clearing levels, and output is less than potential output.
    C. prices adjust to market-clearing levels, and output is greater than potential output.
    D. output is primarily determined by economy-wide spending.
    E. the main effect of total spending is on output.

17. During the period 1960-1999, inflation was at its highest level in the United States during the
    A. boom of 1961-69.
    B. expansion of 1982-90.
    C. expansion of 1990-99.
    D. recession of 1981-82.
    E. recession of 1973-75.

18. Recessions and expansions have a greater impact on
    A. inflation than on unemployment.
    B. frictional unemployment than on cyclical unemployment.

    C. structural unemployment than on cyclical unemployment.
    D. industries that produce durable goods than on service and nondurable goods industries.
    E. industries that produce services and nondurable goods than on durable goods industries.

19. The difference between the total unemployment rate and the natural rate of unemployment
    A. is positive during a recession.
    B. is negative during a recession.
    C. is positive during an expansion.
    D. represents that portion of total unemployment that economists call frictional
unemployment.
    E. represents that portion of total unemployment that economists call structural
unemployment.

20. Online job services have made labor markets more efficient and, thus, have contributed to
    A. a decline in cyclical unemployment.
    B. an increase in cyclical unemployment.
    C. a decline in the natural rate of unemployment.
    D. an increase in the natural rate of unemployment.
    E. an increase in structural and frictional unemployment.

Short Answer Problems
(Answers and solutions are given at the end of the chapter.)

1. Actual Output and Potential Output
This problem utilizes data on real GDP and potential GDP for the United States for the years
1994-1999, in billions of 1992 dollars, and will help you become more familiar with the concept
of output gaps (recessionary and expansionary gaps).

Year	Real GDP	Potential GDP	Output Gap	Expansionary or Recessionary Gap?
1998	$9,611	$9,777		
1999	9,762	9,955		
2000	9,995	10,138		
2001	10,720	10,325		
2002	10,553	10,517		
2003	10,883	10,714		

A. Complete column 4 of the above table by calculating the size of the output gap for 1998
through 2003 (be sure to include a plus sign if a positive gap or a minus sign if a negative gap).
B. In column 5 of the above table, identify whether the output gap was a recessionary gap or an
expansionary gap for each year.

IV. Economic Naturalist Application

In Economic Naturalist 12.1, it is reported that the Business Cycle Dating Committee of the National Bureau of Economic Research determined that a recession began in March 2001. On December 7, 2002, the National Bureau of Economic Research stated, "In 2002, indicators measuring output and income generally have been rising, while employment has been essentially constant. The primary factor accounting for the more favorable performance of income and production relative to employment is the continuation of rapid productivity growth resulting in corresponding growth in real wages."

Based on the information reported in December 2002, explain whether you think the U.S. economy was still in recession during the fourth quarter of 2002?

V. Go to the Web: Graphing Exercises Using Interactive Graphs

Does a Falling Unemployment Rate (at Full Employment) Necessarily Lead to an Expansionary Output Gap?

During 1998-1999 the U.S. unemployment rate fell from 4.7% to 4.1% and reached a 30-year low of 3.9% in April, 2000. Most economists felt that unemployment rates in the 4.0-4.5% range were below the full-employment unemployment rate at the time, although inflation remained low. Inflation often becomes a problem when an expansionary output gap develops, so the fact that inflation rates remained low indicated that the output gap was not increasing. How could the actual unemployment rate continue to fall during 1998-1999 without the expansionary output gap becoming so large that policymakers felt a need to react and slow the economy down?

Answer:

To review an answer to this question, and to learn more about the use of economic theory to analyze this issue (and other macroeconomic issues), please go to the Electronic Learning Session in the Student Center at the Frank/Bernanke web site: http://www.mhhe.com/economics/frankbernanke2.

VI. Self-Test Solutions

Key Terms
1. a
2. i
3. f
4. b

5. d
6. l
7. g
8. j
9. e
10. h
11. c
12. k

Multiple-Choice Questions

1. E
2. D
3. C
4. C
5. A
6. B $9,000 billion times .025 = $225 billion
7. E
8. C
9. D
10. C
11. A
12. D
13. B
14. E
15. B
16. A
17. D
18. C
19. A
20. C

Short Answer Problems

1.
A. and B.

Year	Real GDP	Potential GDP	Output Gap	Expansionary or Recessionary Gap?
1998	$9,611	$9,777	+$166	Expansionary gap
1999	9,762	9,955	+$193	Expansionary gap
2000	9,995	10,138	+$143	Expansionary gap
2001	10,720	10,325	-$395	Recessionary gap
2002	10,553	10,517	-$36	Recessionary gap
2003	10,883	10,714	-$169	Recessionary gap

Chapter 13
Spending and Output
in the Short Run

I. Pretest: What Do You Really Know?
Circle the letter that corresponds to the best answer. (Answers appear immediately after the final question).

1. The two key assumptions of the basic Keynesian model are that aggregate demand _____ and that in the short run firms _____.
   A. is constant; meet demand at preset prices
   B. fluctuates; adjust prices to bring sales into line with capacity
   C. increases with the general level of prices; meet demand at preset prices
   D. is constant; adjust prices to bring sales into line with capacity
   E. fluctuates; meet demand at preset prices

2. Firms do not change prices frequently because
   A. there are legal prohibitions against doing so.
   B. it is easier to change the quantity of capital used in production.
   C. it is costly to do so.
   D. customers will refuse to patronize firms that change prices frequently.
   E. managers are lazy.

3. If firms sell more output than expected, planned investment
   A. is greater than actual investment.
   B. is less than actual investment.
   C. equals actual investment.
   D. equals zero.
   E. equals aggregate demand.

4. Dave's Mirror Company expects to sell $2,000,000 worth of mirrors and to produce $2,250,000 worth of mirrors in the coming year. The company purchases $500,000 of new equipment during the year. Sales for the year turn out to be $1,900,000. Actual investment by Dave's Mirror Company equals _____ and planned investment equals _____.
   A. $500,000; $500,000
   B. $500,000; $750,000

C. $750,000; $850,000
D. $850,000; $500,000
E. $850,000; $750,000

5. The consumption function is a relationship between consumption and
   A. aggregate demand.
   B. total spending.
   C. investment.
   D. its determinants, such as disposable income.
   E. unplanned changes in spending, particularly inventory investment.

6. If consumption increases by $90 when after-tax disposable income increases by $100, the marginal propensity to consume equals
   A. 0.1
   B. 0.9
   C. 1.0
   D. 90
   E. 100

7. Autonomous expenditure is the portion of planned aggregate expenditure that
   A. equals aggregate output.
   B. equals planned spending.
   C. equals induced aggregate demand.
   D. is determined within the model.
   E. is determined outside the model.

8. In Macroland autonomous consumption equals 200, the marginal propensity to consume equals 0.6, net taxes are fixed at 50, planned investment is fixed at 100, government purchases are fixed at 200, and net exports are fixed at 30. Short-run equilibrium output in this economy equals
   A. 1,100
   B. 1,175
   C. 1,250
   D. 1,325
   E. 1,400

9. If planned aggregate expenditure in an economy can be written as: AD = 4000 + .8Y, what is the short-run equilibrium level of output in this economy?
   A. 5,000
   B. 5,800
   C. 9,000
   D. 20,000
   E. 25,000

10. For an economy starting from potential output, a decrease in planned investment in the short run results in a(n)
   A. expansionary output gap.
   B. recessionary output gap.
   C. increase in potential output.
   D. decrease in potential output.
   E. increase in cyclical unemployment.

Solutions and Feedback to Pretest
For each question you incorrectly answered, we strongly recommend taking the time to review the appropriate material before continuing. In the table below, the relevant textbook pages are listed for each question as well as the pertinent Learning Objective from the following Key Point Review.

Correct Answer	Textbook Page Numbers	Learning Objective
1. E	p. 330	1
2. C	pp. 330 - 31	1
3. A	pp. 332 - 33	3
4. E	pp. 332 - 33	3
5. B	pp. 333 - 35	4
6. B	pp. 333 - 35	4
7. E	p. 337	5
8. C	pp. 338 - 41	6
9. D	pp. 338 - 41	6
10. B	pp. 341 - 42	7

II. Key Point Review
In this chapter, the basic Keynesian model (also known as the Keynesian cross) is developed showing how recessions and expansions may arise from fluctuations in aggregate spending. The chapter first presents the two key assumptions of the model, then explains the important concept of total, or aggregate, planned spending in the economy. After showing how planned aggregate expenditure helps to determine the level of output, the use of government policies to reduce or eliminate output gaps is discussed.

Learning Objective 1: Identify the key assumption of the model.
The Keynesian model is based on the ideas first developed by John Maynard Keynes (1883-1946) and published in *The General Theory of Employment, Interest and Money* (1936). The key assumption of the basic Keynesian model is that, in the short run, firms meet the demand for their products at preset prices. Firms change prices only if the benefits of doing so outweigh the **menu costs**, (i.e., the costs of changing prices).

Note: the decision by a firm whether to change price is an application of the cost-benefit principle. Firms will only change the price of a product if the marginal benefit is at least equal to the marginal cost

Learning Objective 2: Define planned aggregate expenditure (PAE) and identify the four components of PAE.
The most important concept of the basic Keynesian model is planned aggregate expenditure. **Planned aggregate expenditure** (PAE) is the total planned spending on final goods and services. PAE is composed of four components: (1) consumer expenditures, or simply consumption (C), is spending by households on final goods and services; (2) investment (I) is spending by firms on new capital goods, residential investment, and increases in inventories; (3) government purchases (G) is spending by the federal, state and local governments on goods and services; and (4) net exports (NX), or exports minus imports, is sales of domestically produced goods and services to foreigners less purchases by domestic residents of goods and services produced abroad.

Learning Objective 3: Explain why planned spending may differ from actual spending.
Planned spending (or PAE) may differ from actual spending. If, for example, a firm sells more of its output than it planned to sell, actual investment will be less than planned investment and total actual spending will be greater than total planned spending. Assuming that actual spending for consumption, government purchases, and net exports equals planned spending, but that actual investment may not equal planned investment, the equation for planned aggregate expenditure is $PAE = C + I^p + G + NX$, where I^p is planned investment spending.

Note: If a firms actual sales are greater than its expected sales, actual investment will be less than planned investment because there will be an unexpected decrease in inventories. Since changes in inventory are one component of investment, an unexpected decrease will reduce actual investment below the planned level of investment.

Learning Objective 4: Define consumption function and marginal propensity to consume.
Consumption, the largest component of *PAE*, is affected by many factors, the most important being after-tax, or disposable, income. The relationship between consumption spending and its determinants is referred to as the **consumption function** and is expressed by the equation $C = \overline{C} + c(Y - T)$, where $\overline{C}$ is a constant term intended to capture factors other than disposable income, $(Y - T)$ represents disposable income, and c is a fixed number called the marginal propensity to consume. The **marginal propensity to consume**, or MPC, is the amount by which consumption rises when disposable income rises by one dollar, and is greater than 0 but less than 1 (i.e., $0 < c < 1$). The consumption function can also be show graphically, in which case $\overline{C}$ represents the intercept of the consumption function on the vertical axis and the MPC is the slope of the consumption function. The consumption function indicates that as disposable income rises, consumption spending will increase, but by a lesser amount.

Learning Objective 5: Explain the relationship between the consumption function and planned aggregate expenditure.

Incorporating the consumption function into the equation for planned aggregate expenditure results in the expanded equation $PAE = [C + c(Y - T)] + I^p + G + NX$. Grouping together those terms that depend on output (Y), and those that do not, yields the equation $PAE = [C + cT + I^p + G + NX] + cY$. This equation captures the key idea that as planned aggregate expenditure changes real output changes with it, in the same direction. It also shows that planned aggregate expenditure can be divided into two parts, one portion that is determined outside the model called **autonomous expenditure** ($[C + cT + I^p + G + NX]$), and a second portion that is determined within the model (because it depends on output) called **induced expenditure** (cY).

Hint: It will be important that you are able to calculate changes in the amount of autonomous expenditure because changes in autonomous expenditure cause changes in the equilibrium level of output. If you do not know the components of autonomous expenditure, you will not be able to calculate changes in autonomous expenditure and, thus, will not be able to determine the impact on the equilibrium level of output.

Learning Objective 6: Define short-run equilibrium output.

In the basic Keynesian model, the **short-run equilibrium output** is the level at which output, Y, equals planned aggregate expenditure, PAE, and is the level of output that prevails during the period in which prices are predetermined. The short-run equilibrium output can be determined numerically by comparing possible levels for short-run equilibrium output to the value of planned aggregate expenditure at each level of output. The short-run equilibrium output is determined where $Y = PAE$, or equivalently $Y - PAE = 0$. The short-run equilibrium output can also be determined graphically where the 45° line intersects the expenditure line. If output is less (greater) than the equilibrium level in the short run, when prices are pre-set and firms are committed to meeting their customers' demand, output will rise (fall).

Learning Objective 7: Explain how a decrease in planned spending can lead to a recession.

A decrease in one or more of the components of autonomous planned aggregate expenditure will cause short-run equilibrium output to fall. When the short-run equilibrium output is less than the potential output, the result is a recessionary gap. According to the basic Keynesian model, inadequate spending is an important cause of recessions in the economy.

Learning Objective 8: Define the income-expenditure multiplier.

A decrease in one or more of the components of autonomous planned aggregate expenditure will cause short-run equilibrium output to fall. The effect of a one-unit increase or decrease in autonomous planned spending on the short-run equilibrium output is called the **income-expenditure multiplier,** or the multiplier for short. In the basic Keynesian model, the multiplier is inversely related to the marginal propensity to consume.

Learning Objective 9: Discuss the use of fiscal policy to stabilize planned spending.
To fight recessions caused by insufficient planned aggregate expenditure, policymakers can use stabilization policies. **Stabilization policies** are government policies that are used to affect planned aggregate expenditure, with the objective of eliminating output gaps. There are two major types of stabilization policy, monetary policy and fiscal policy. This chapter focuses on fiscal policy, i.e., government spending and taxes. Keynes felt that changes in government spending were probably the most effective tool for reducing or eliminating output gaps. He argued that a recessionary gap could be eliminated by increases in government spending. Alternatively, a decrease in taxes (payments from the private sector to government) could eliminate a recessionary gap. Government spending can be in the form of government purchases of goods and services or transfer payments (payments from government to the private sector). Changes in government purchases directly change the amount of PAE, whereas transfer payments and taxes only indirectly change PAE by altering the amount of disposable income. The change in PAE is equal to the change in taxes (or transfer payments) times the MPC. Because the MPC is a fraction, the change in taxes or transfer payments must be larger than the change in government purchases to cause the same change in PAE.

Learning Objective 10: Discuss three qualifications related to the use of fiscal policy as a stabilization tool.
While the basic Keynesian model suggests that fiscal policy can be used quite precisely to eliminate output gaps, in the real world it is more complicated than that. Using fiscal policy as a stabilization tool is complicated by the fact that it may affect potential output as well as planned aggregate expenditure. Government spending, for example, on investments in public capital (e.g., roads, airports, and schools) can play a major role in the growth of potential output. Taxes and transfer payments may affect the incentives, and thus the economic behavior, of households and firms that, in turn, affect potential output. A second qualification is the need to avoid large and persistent government budget deficits. The need to keep deficits under control may make it more difficult to increase government spending or cut taxes to fight a recession. The third qualification is that fiscal policy is not always flexible enough to be useful for stabilization. Changes in government spending or taxation must usually go through a lengthy legislative process making it difficult to respond in a timely way to economic conditions. In addition, policymakers have many objectives besides stabilizing planned aggregate expenditure.

III. Self-Test

Key Terms
Match the term in the right-hand column with the appropriate definitions in the left-hand column by placing the letter of the term in the blank in front of its definition. (Answers are given at the end of the chapter.)

1. _____ The tendency of changes in asset prices to affect households' wealth and thus their spending on consumption goods.

a. automatic stabilizers

2. _____ The portion of planned aggregate expenditure that depends on output.

b. autonomous expenditure

3. _____ The portion of planned aggregate expenditure that is

c. consumption

independent of output.   function
4. ____ Government policies that are used to affect planned   d. contractionary
aggregate expenditure, with the objective of eliminating output   policies
gaps.
5. ____ The level of output at which output equals planned   e. expansionary
aggregate expenditure.   policies
6. ____ Government policy actions designed to reduce planned   f. induced
spending and output.   expenditure
7. ____ The costs of changing prices.   g. income-
                                                                     expenditure multiplier
8. ____ The effect of a 1-unit increase in autonomous   h. marginal
expenditure on short-run equilibrium output.   propensity to consume
                                                                     (MPC)
9. ____ Total planned spending on final goods and services.   i.   menu costs
10.____ The relationship between consumption spending and its   j.   planned aggregate
determinants, in particular, disposable (after-tax) income.   expenditure
11.____ The amount by which consumption rises when   k. short-run
disposable income rise by one dollar.   equilibrium output
12.____ Provisions in law that provide automatic increases in   l.   stabilization
government spending or decreases in taxes when real output   policies
declines..
13.____ Government policy actions intended to increase planned   m. wealth effect
spending and output.

Multiple-Choice Questions
Circle the letter that corresponds to the best answer. (Answers are given at the end of the chapter.)

1. Which of the following is the key assumption of the basic Keynesian model?
    A. Total spending fluctuates.
    B. In the short run, firms meet the demand for their products at preset prices.
    C. In the long run, firms meet the demand for the products at preset prices.
    D. In the short run, firms adjust prices to changes in planned aggregate expenditure so as to clear the market.
    E. In the long run, firms adjust prices to changes in planned aggregate expenditure so as to clear the market.

2. When firms apply the core principle of cost-benefit analysis to price-changing decisions, they change the prices of their goods if
    A. menu costs are greater than or equal to the benefits of changing prices.
    B. menu costs are greater than or equal to the additional revenue derived from changing prices.
    C. additional revenue derived from changing prices is less than the menu costs.
    D. additional revenue derived from changing prices is greater than the menu costs.
    E. additional revenue derived from changing prices is less than or equal to the menu costs.

3. In *The General Theory of Employment, Interest, and Money*, John Maynard Keynes explained
   A. how economies always operate at the natural rate of employment.
   B. the causes of expansionary gaps and recommended the use of monetary policy to combat the resulting high inflation.
   C. how economies can remain at low levels of output for long periods and recommended increased government spending to combat the resulting high unemployment.
   D. that attempts to extract large reparation payments from Germany after World War I would prevent economic recovery of Germany and likely lead to another war.
   E. the key elements of the post-WWII international monetary and financial institutions.

4. Planned aggregate expenditure is the sum of desired or planned
   A. consumption expenditures, investment, government purchases, and net exports.
   B. consumption expenditures, investment, government purchases, and exports.
   C. consumption expenditures, investment, government purchases, and net imports.
   D. consumption expenditures, net investment, government purchases, and net exports.
   E. consumption expenditures, net investment, government expenditures, and net exports.

5. If a firms' actual sales are greater than expected sales
   A. actual inventories will be greater than planned inventories, and actual investment will be greater than planned investment.
   B. actual inventories will be less than planned inventories, and actual investment will be less than planned investment.
   C. actual inventories will be greater than planned inventories, and actual investment will be less than planned investment.
   D. actual inventories will be less than planned inventories, and actual investment will be greater than planned investment.
   E. planned inventories will be less than actual inventories, and planned investment will be greater than actual investment.

6. A decrease in consumers' disposable income will cause a(n)
   A. decrease in the consumption function and an increase in output.
   B. increase in the consumption function and a decrease in output.
   C. decrease in the consumption function and an increase in planned aggregate expenditure.
   D. increase in the consumption function and an increase in planned aggregate expenditure.
   E. decrease in the consumption function and a decrease in planned aggregate expenditure.

7. If autonomous consumption equals $250 billion, the marginal propensity to consume (MPC) is .6, investment equals $180 billion, government purchases equal $75 billion, taxes equal $200, and net exports equal minus $40 billion, the planned aggregate expenditure equation is
   A. PAE = $250 billion + .6Y
   B. PAE = $585 billion + .6Y
   C. PAE = $505 billion + .6Y
   D. PAE = $625 billion + .6Y
   E. PAE = $345 billion + .6Y

8. If, in the short run, real output is less than the equilibrium level of output, firms will respond by
   A. increasing the price of their products.
   B. decreasing the price of their products.
   C. increasing their production.
   D. decreasing their production.
   E. producing the same amount of output.

9. If the consumption function is C = $400 + .75Y, then the MPC equals
   A. $400.
   B. .25.
   C. $400 + .75.
   D. .75.
   E. 4.

10. John Maynard Keynes believed that the most effective stabilization policy was
    A. changes in government spending to reduce or eliminate output gaps.
    B. monetary policy to reduce or eliminate expansionary gaps.
    C. changes in government spending to reduce or eliminate recessionary gaps, but monetary policy to reduce or eliminate expansionary gaps.
    D. changes in taxes to reduce or eliminate output gaps.
    E. the self-correcting process of the market to reduce or eliminate output gaps.

11. The largest single component of planned aggregate expenditures is
    A. government spending.
    B. consumption spending.
    C. investment spending.
    D. export spending.
    E. import spending.

12. The use of fiscal policy to eliminate output gaps is complicated by the fact that fiscal policy
    A. is more flexible than monetary policy.
    B. only affects planned aggregate expenditure, but has no effect on potential output.
    C. affects both planned aggregate expenditure and potential output.
    D. does not take into account the effects that automatic stabilizers have on potential output.
    E. includes not only government purchases, but also transfer payments and taxation.

13. If the marginal propensity to consume increases, the income expenditure multiplier
    A. increases.
    B. decreases.
    C. remains unchanged.
    D. decreases by a smaller amount.
    E. increases by a larger amount.

14. Planned spending equals actual spending for households, governments, and foreigners in the basic Keynesian model, but for businesses
    A. planned spending equals actual inventories.
    B. planned spending equals planned inventories.
    C. actual investment may differ from planned investment.
    D. actual investment is always greater than planned investment.
    E. actual investment is always less than planned investment

15. The portion of planned aggregate expenditure that is determined within the model is called induced expenditure and includes
    A. that part of household consumption that is dependent upon income.
    B. all of household consumption.
    C. household consumption and investment spending.
    D. household consumption, investment spending, and government purchases.
    E. household consumption, investment spending, government purchases, and net exports.

16. The short-run equilibrium in the basic Keynesian model occurs where
    A. actual inventories are greater than the level planned by businesses.
    B. actual inventories are less than the level planned by businesses.
    C. planned aggregate expenditure equals potential output.
    D. planned aggregate expenditure equals output.
    E. planned aggregate expenditure is greater than output.

17. In the basic Keynesian model, when planned aggregate expenditure equals output
    A. inventories are zero.
    B. consumption equals investment.
    C. unplanned changes in inventories are positive.
    D. unplanned changes in inventories equal zero.
    E. unplanned changes in inventories are negative.

18. If, in the short run, output is greater than the equilibrium level of output, firms will respond by
    A. increasing the price of their products.
    B. decreasing the price of their products.
    C. producing the same amount of output.
    D. increasing their production.
    E. decreasing their production.

19. A $100 increase in transfer payments or a $100 decrease in taxes will cause
    A. a smaller increase in planned aggregate expenditure than a $100 increase in government purchases.
    B. a larger increase in planned aggregate expenditure than a $100 increase in government purchases.
    C. the same increase in planned aggregate expenditure as would a $100 increase in government purchases.

D. a smaller decrease in planned aggregate expenditure than a $100 increase in government purchases.
E. a larger decrease in planned aggregate expenditure than a $100 increase in government purchases.

20. Fiscal policy is not always flexible enough to be useful for economic stabilization because
    A. automatic stabilizers counteract the stabilizing features of government spending and taxation.
    B. budget deficits are unconstitutional.
    C. the legislative process allows policymakers inadequate time to determine the appropriate level of government spending and taxation.
    D. it affects both planned aggregate expenditure and potential output.
    E. the only effects of fiscal policy that matter are its effects on potential output.

Short Answer Problems
(Answers and solutions are given at the end of the chapter.)

1. The Consumption Function and Planned Aggregate Expenditure
This problem is designed to help you understand the relationship between the consumption function and planned aggregate expenditure. You will be asked to graph the consumption function, write the algebraic equation for planned aggregate expenditure, and differentiate between autonomous and induced expenditure.

A. On the graph below, plot the consumption function curve (label it C) for disposable income levels $0 to $700, assuming C = $175 billion, the marginal propensity to consume (MPC) equals .75, and taxes equal $100 billion.

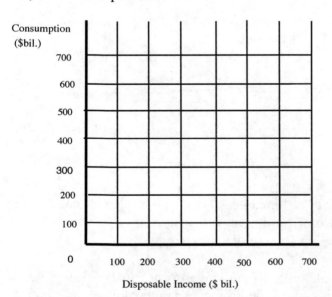

B. Assume that planned investment spending equals $50 billion, government purchases are $75 billion, and net exports equal –$75 billion. The algebraic equation for the planned aggregate expenditure curve would be PAE = $ _____ billion + _____ (Y - $_____ billion) + $

_____ billion + $_____ billion + $_____ billion. Combining the autonomous portions of PAE would result in a simplified equation, PAE = $_____ billion + _____ Y.

C. Plot the planned aggregate expenditure curve on the above graph and label it PAE.

D. Autonomous expenditure equals $_____ billion, and is graphically represented where the planned aggregate expenditure curve intersects the (vertical/ horizontal) _____ axis.

E. When disposable income equals $400 billion, the induced expenditure equals $_____ billion.

2. Numerical Determination of Short-run Equilibrium Output

The focus of this problem is the determination of the short-run equilibrium output within the framework of a numerical table.

(1) Output (Y)	(2) Planned aggregate expenditure	(3) Y– PAE	(4) Y = PAE?
$3,000			
3,500			
4,000			
4,500			
5,000			
5,500			
6,000			

A. Assume that planned aggregate expenditure is determined by the equation PAE = $500 + .9 Y. Complete column 2 of the table by calculating the amount of planned aggregate expenditure when output equals $3,000 to $6,000.

B. Complete column 3 of the table by calculating the difference between output and planned aggregate expenditure when output equals $3,000 to $6,000.

C. Complete column 4 of the table by determining whether or not Y = PAE. The equilibrium level of output equals $_____ .

D. If output equals $ 3,500, firms will (increase/decrease) _____ the level of output.

E. If output equals $ 6,000, firms will (increase/decrease) _____ the level of output.

3. The Basic Keynesian Model

This problem is designed to help you understand the fundamentals of the basic Keynesian model. You will determine the equilibrium level of income (or output) and analyze the effects of changes in investment spending on the equilibrium level of income (or output).

A. Assume the consumption function is C = $200 billion + .8Y, investment equals $ 150 billion, government purchases equal $200 billion, taxes equal $100 billion, and net exports equals minus $70 billion. Using this information, derive the aggregate expenditure function. PAE = $_____ billion + _____ Y.

B. On the graph below, plot the planned aggregate expenditure curve for level of output ranging from $0 billion to $5,000 billion (label the curve PAE).

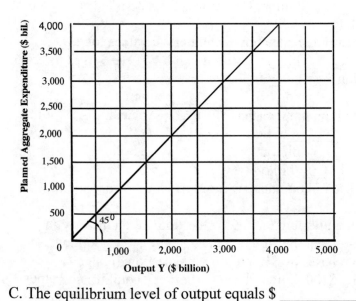

Output Y ($ billion)

C. The equilibrium level of output equals $ _____ billion.

D. If the potential output (Y*) equals $2,500, there would now be a (recessionary/ expansionary) _____ gap in the economy.

E. If firms produce $3,000 billion of output, planned aggregate expenditure would equal $_____ billion. As a result, firms would have $_____ billion of goods they intended to sell but didn't. This would cause firms to (increase / decrease) _____ their level of output.

Note: Questions 3F – 3H are based on information in Appendix B of the textbook chapter.

F. The MPC equals _____ and the multiplier equals _____ .

G. If investment spending decreases by $100 billion, the planned aggregate expenditure curve will shift (upward / downward) _____ and the equilibrium output will (increase / decrease) _____ by an amount equal to the change in planned aggregate expenditure times the multiplier.

H. On the graph above, draw the planned aggregate expenditure curve after a $100-billion decrease in investment spending (label it PAE₁). The new equilibrium output would equal $_____ billion.

4. Solving the Basic Keynesian Model Numerically
(Based on material in Appendix A of the textbook chapter.)
This problem uses algebraic equations to determine the short-run equilibrium output. You will derive the planned aggregate expenditure equation and, employing the equation for the short-run equilibrium condition, calculate the short-run equilibrium output, and determine the effect of changes in government purchases, taxes, and transfer payments of the short-run equilibrium output.

Use the following set of equations to answer the questions below:
$C = \$400$ billion $+ .75(Y - T)$
$T = \$200$ billion
$I^P = \$250$ billion
$G = \$300$ billion

NX = $50 billion

A. Using the information above, substitute into the equation the numerical values for each component of planned aggregate expenditure. Y= $_____ billion + _____(Y – $_____ billion) + $_____ billion + $_____ billion + $_____ billion.
B. After simplifying, that equation yields the equation PAE = $_____ billion + _____Y.
C. The definition of short-run equilibrium output implies that Y = PAE. Replacing PAE with the equation found in Question 4B yields Y = $_____ billion + _____Y.
D. Now solve for Y in Y – ____ Y = $_____ billion, or Y = $_____ billion.
E. Thus, the equilibrium output equals $_____ billion.
F. If government purchases decrease by $100 billion, the new short-run equilibrium output will equal $_____ billion.
G. Starting from the level of the short-run equilibrium output in Question 4E, an increase in taxation of $100 will result in a new short-run equilibrium output of $_____ billion.
H. If, instead of decreasing government purchases by $100 billion in Question 4F, the government decreased transfer payments by $100 billion, the new short-run equilibrium output would equal $_____ billion.
I. In comparing the answers to Questions 4F-H, it is apparent that a change in government purchases has a (greater/lesser/equal) _____ effect on the short-run equilibrium output than does an equal change in transfer payments or taxation.

IV. Economic Naturalist Application

Economic Naturalist 13.4 discusses the impact of the Japanese recession on its neighboring countries in East Asia. The Japanese economy's slump during the 1990s has resulted in less household and business spending on imports from these economies and, therefore, autonomous expenditures have declined. The fall in autonomous expenditures has led to a recessionary gap in those economies. Based on the textbook discussion of stabilization policy within the context of the basic Keynesian model, explain what the appropriate fiscal policy would be to close the recessionary gap. Also, discuss the limitations of the use of fiscal policy to close the recessionary gap.

V. Go to the Web: Graphing Exercises Using Interactive Graphs

Does the Stock Market Affect the Economy?

Alan Greenspan, the Chairman of the Board of Governors of the Federal Reserve, argued in the spring of 2000 that rising stock prices in the U.S. stock market were increasing consumer wealth, which in turn was fueling increased consumer expenditures and threatening to push the economy beyond its potential output level. According to the basic Keynesian model, were Greenspan's arguments plausible? If so, what could the government do to keep the economy from operating beyond its potential output level?
Answer:

To review an answer to this question, and to learn more about the use of economic theory to analyze this issue (and other macroeconomic issues), please go to the Electronic Learning Session in the Student Center at the Frank/Bernanke web site: http://www.mhhe.com/economics/frankbernanke2.

VI. Self-Test Solutions

Key Terms
1. m
2. f
3. b
4. l
5. k
6. d
7. i
8. g
9. j
10. c
11. h
12. a
13. e

Multiple-Choice Questions
1. B
2. D
3. C
4. A
5. B
6. E
7. E $250 billion + [.6(Y - $200 billion)] + $180 billion + $75 billion + (-$40 billion) = $345 billion + .6Y
8. C
9. D
10. A
11. B
12. C
13. B
14. C
15. A
16. D
17. D
18. E
19. A
20. B

Short Answer Problems

1.

A.

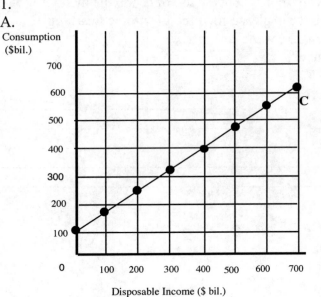

B. $175 billion + .75(Y - $100 billion) + $50 billion + $75 billion + (-$75) billion;
$150 billion + .75Y

C.

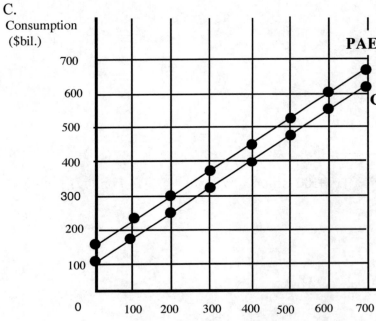

D. $150 billion (= $175 billion - $75 billion + $50 billion + 75 billion - $75 billion); vertical
E. $300 billion (= .75 x $400 billion)

2. A. B.

(1) Output (Y)	(2) Planned Aggregate Expenditure	(3) Y– PAE	(4) Y = PAE?
$3,000	$3,200	$-200	No
3,500	3,650	-150	No
4,000	4,100	-100	No
4,500	4,550	-50	No
5,000	5,000	0	Yes
5,500	5,550	50	No
6,000	6,100	100	No

C. $5,000
D. increase
E. decrease

3.
A. PAE = $400 billion + .8Y
B.

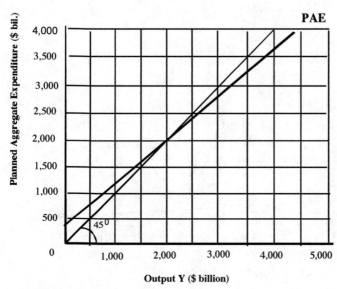

C. $2,000 billion
D. recessionary gap; $500
E. $2,800 billion (= $400 billion + .8($3,000 billion); $200 billion (Y – PAE, or $3,000 billion – $2,800 billion); decrease

F. .8 ; 5 $(=\dfrac{1}{1-.8}=\dfrac{1}{.2})$

G. downward; decrease

H.

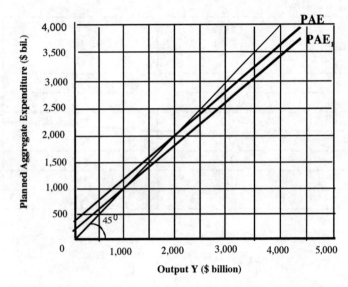

; $1,500 billion (The change in equilibrium output is – $100 billion x 5 = – $500 billion. Subtracting the change in equilibrium output from the initial equilibrium output, $2,000 billion - $500 billion, gives us the new equilibrium output of $1,500 billion.)

4.
A. $400 billion + .75 (Y - $200 billion) + $250 billion + $300 billion + $50 billion
B. AD = $850 billion + .75Y
C. Y = $850 billion + .75Y;
D. Y= $3,400 billion (The solution is found by first moving the .75 Y to the left side of the equation and subtracting it from Y. In equation form it is written, Y – .75 Y = $850 billion. Reducing the left-hand side yields the equation, .25Y = $850 billion. Next, divide both sides of the equation by .25. This gives us Y = $850 billion / .25, and dividing $850 billion by .25 equals $3,400 billion. Thus Y= $3,400 billion)
E. $3,400 billion
F. $3,000 billion (Y – .75Y =$750 billion, or .25Y = $750 billion, thus Y= $3,000 billion)
G. $3,100 billion (Y – .75 Y = $675, or .25Y = $775 billion, thus Y = $3,100 billion)
H. $3,100 billion (the effect of a decrease in transfer payments is the same as an increase in taxation, and thus the numerical derivation is identical to the answer to 4G).
I. greater

Chapter 14
Stabilizing the Economy:
The Role of the Fed

I. Pretest: What Do You Really Know?

Circle the letter that corresponds to the best answer. (Answers appear immediately after the final question).

1. Monetary policy is _____ flexible than fiscal policy because monetary policy changes are made by _____, while fiscal policy changes must be made by _____.
    A. more; the FOMC; legislative action
    B. more; legislative action; the FOMC
    C. more; the President; legislative action
    D. less; the FOMC; the President
    E. less; the President; legislative action

2. The benefit of holding money is _____, while the opportunity cost of holding money is _____.
    A. the nominal interest rate; the fees charged by banks
    B. the nominal interest rate; its usefulness in carrying out transactions
    C. increased income; lost purchasing power
    D. its usefulness in carrying out transactions; the nominal interest rate
    E. its usefulness in carrying out transactions; the price of wallets and billfolds

3. The following table shows Alex's estimated annual benefits of holding different amounts of money.

Average money holdings ($)	Total benefit ($)
300	30
400	39
500	46
600	51
700	54

    How much money will Alex hold if the nominal interest rate is 8 percent? (Assume she wants her money holdings to be in multiples of $100.)
    A. $300
    B. $400
    C. $500

D. $600
E. $700

4. Lower real income ____ the demand for money, and a lower price level ___ the demand for money.
   A. increases; increases
   B. increases; decreases
   C. increases; does not change
   D. decreases; decreases
   E. decreases; increases

5. Which of the following would be expected to increase the U.S. demand for money?
   A. Competition among brokers lowers the commission charge for selling bonds or stocks.
   B. The economy enters a recession.
   C. Political instability increases dramatically in developing nations.
   D. On-line banking allows customers to transfer funds between checking and stock mutual funds 24 hours a day.
   E. Financial investors become less concerned about the riskiness of stocks.

6. If the nominal interest rate is below the equilibrium value, then money demand is _____ than money supply, bond prices will ____, and the nominal interest rate will ____.
   A. greater; fall; increase
   B. greater; fall; decrease
   C. greater; rise; increase
   D. less; fall; increase
   E. less; rise; decrease

7. If the Fed wishes to increase nominal interest rates, it must engage in an open market ____ of bonds that ____ the money supply.
   A. sale; increases
   B. sale; decreases
   C. sale; does not change
   D. purchase; increases
   E. purchase; decreases

8. The Fed's control over real interest rates is
   A. absolute
   B. greater than its control over nominal interest rates
   C. less than its control over nominal interest rate
   D. impossible
   E. unimportant

9. The interest rate that commercial banks charge each other for very short-term loans is called the
   A. prime rate.
   B. federal funds rate.

   C. Federal Reserve discount rate.
   D. commercial paper rate.
   E. bank loan rate.

10. A lower real interest rate _____ investment spending and _____ consumption spending.
   A. increases; increases
   B. increases; decreases
   C. does not change; does not change
   D. decreases; increases
   E. decreases; decreases

Solutions and Feedback to Pretest
For each question you incorrectly answered, we strongly recommend taking the time to review the appropriate material before continuing. In the table below, the relevant textbook pages are listed for each question as well as the pertinent Learning Objective from the following Key Point Review.

Correct Answer	Textbook Page Numbers	Learning Objective
1. A	pp. 377-78	5
2. D	pp.368-69	2
3. D	pp. 368-69	2
4. D	pp. 371-75	3
5. C	pp.371-75	3
6. A	pp. 375-76	4
7. B	pp. 377-78	5
8. C	pp. 379-80	7
9. B	pp. 378-79	6
10. A	pp. 381-83	8

II. Key Point Review

This chapter examines the workings of monetary policy, one of the two major types of stabilization policy. The chapter begins with a discussion of how the Fed uses its ability to control the money supply to influence nominal and real interest rates. The chapter concludes by building on the analysis of the basic Keynesian model to explain the effects of monetary policy and interest rates on planned aggregate expenditures and short-run equilibrium output.

Learning Objective 1: Define demand for money.
As explained in an earlier chapter, the Fed uses three tools to control the money supply. This chapter shows that the Fed's control of the money supply is tantamount to controlling nominal interest rates. The nominal interest rate is the price of money and is determined by the supply and demand for money. The **demand for money** is the result of choices made by households and businesses. The demand for money is the amount of wealth an individual chooses to hold in the form of money. Households and businesses demand money to carry out transactions (i.e., use it as a medium of exchange) and as a way of holding wealth (i.e., the store of value function of money).

> **Hint:** When economists talk about household and business demand for money they are **not** asking how much money you want. The answer to that question is always "more." The demand for money refers to how much of your wealth you want to hold in the form of money (and, by implication, how much of your wealth will be held in nonmoney forms).

Learning Objective 2: Define portfolio allocation decision and explain how it relates to the demand for money.

There are almost an infinite number of forms in which wealth can be held. The decision about the forms in which to hold ones wealth is called the **portfolio allocation decision**. How much money one chooses to hold is based on the costs and benefits of holding money. The opportunity cost of holding money is the interest that could have been earned if the person had chosen to hold interest-bearing assets instead of money. The higher the prevailing interest rate, the greater the opportunity cost of holding money, and hence the less money individuals and businesses will demand. The principle benefit of holding money is its usefulness in carrying out transactions. The amount of money demanded to carry out transactions is affected at the macroeconomic level by real output and the price level. An increase in aggregate real output or income raises the quantity of goods and services that people and businesses want to buy and, thus, raises the demand for money. The higher the price of goods and services, the more dollars needed to make a given set of transactions and, therefore, the higher the demand for money.

Learning Objective 3: Discuss macroeconomic factors that affect the demand for money and the effects of changes on the money demand curve.

Macroeconomists are primarily interested in the aggregate, or economy-wide, demand for money, represented by the money demand curve. The **money demand curve** relates the aggregate quantity of money demand, M, to the nominal interest rate, i. Because an increase in the nominal interest rate increases the opportunity cost of holding money, which reduces the quantity of money demanded, the money demand curve slopes down. An increase in real output or the price level will cause the money demand curve to increase (shift to the right), while a fall in either will cause it to decrease (shift to the left). Other factors, such as technological and financial advances, also cause the money demand curve to shift.

Learning Objective 4: Identify the money market equilibrium.

The supply of money is controlled by the Federal Reserve (the central bank of the United States). Its primary tool for controlling the money supply is open-market operations. Because the Fed fixes the supply of money, the money supply curve is a vertical line that intercepts the horizontal axis at the quantity of money chosen by the Fed. The equilibrium in the market for money occurs at the intersection of the supply and demand for money curves. The equilibrium amount of money in circulation is the amount of money the Fed chooses to supply. The equilibrium nominal interest rate is the interest rate at which the quantity of money demanded by the public equals the fixed supply of money made available by the Fed.

Note: Money is a commodity and can be exchanged in the market. Like any other goods, it can satisfy wants and, therefore, households and businesses demand money. Unlike most other goods, the supply of money is controlled by the Fed to achieve public goals rather than to maximize profits. The money market, thus, behaves much like any other commodity market, but also has some unique features.

Learning Objective 5: Explain how monetary policy is used to control nominal interest rates.

When the Fed increases the money supply by purchasing government bonds from the public, it drives up the price of bonds and, thus, lowers the equilibrium nominal interest rate. When the Fed decreases the money supply through open-market sales of government bonds to the public, the price of bonds is driven down and, therefore, the equilibrium nominal interest rate must rise.

Note: Recall from our earlier discussion, there is an inverse relationship between bond prices and interest rates, i.e., when bond prices rise, market interest rates will go down.

Learning Objective 6: Define the federal funds rate and explain why the Fed has focused on it.

Although there are thousands of different interest rates determined in the financial markets, the textbook authors use the phrase *the nominal interest rate* to refer to an average measure of these interest rates because they tend to rise and fall together. Of all the market interest rates, the one that is most closely watched by the public, politicians, and the media, however, is the federal funds rate. The **federal funds rate** is the interest rate commercial banks charge each other for very short-term (usually overnight) loans. It is closely watched because for the past 35 years, the Fed has expressed its policies in terms of a target value for the federal funds rate. Because interest rates tend to move together, an action by the Fed to change the federal funds rate generally causes other interest rates to change in the same direction. The tendency of interest rates to move together, however, is not an exact relationship. This means that the Fed's control over other interest rates is somewhat less precise than its control over the federal funds rate.

Learning Objective 7: Discuss the Fed's ability to control the real rate of interest.

Similarly, the Fed's control over real interest rates is less complete than its control over nominal interest rates. The real interest rate equals the nominal interest rate minus the rate of inflation. Because inflation tends to change relatively slowly in response to changes in policy or economic conditions, actions by the Fed to change nominal interest rates allows it to control real interest rates in the short run. In the long run, however, the inflation rate and other variables will adjust, and the balance of saving and investment will determine the real interest.

> **Note:** The reason it is important that the Fed be able to influence (if not control) changes in real (not nominal) interest rates is that that causes changes in economic behavior. Therefore, if the Fed is to be effective in formulating and implementing monetary policy it must be able to influence real interest rates.

Learning Objective 8: Explain how interest rates affect consumption and investment spending, aggregate demand, and short-run equilibrium output.
Because the Fed can control the money supply and interest rates (at least, in the short run), monetary policy can be used to eliminate output gaps and stabilize the economy. Consumption and planned investment spending are inversely related to real interest rates, that is, a decrease in real interest rates will cause consumption and planned investment spending to increase. Because consumption and planned investment spending are components of planned aggregate expenditures, changes in real interest rates cause changes in planned aggregate expenditures. By adjusting real interest rates, the Fed can move planned aggregate expenditures in the desired direction. For example, an expansionary monetary policy, or monetary easing, is a reduction in interest rates by the Fed, made with the intention of reducing a recessionary gap. If the economy faces a recessionary gap, the Fed could reduce real interest rates to stimulate consumption and investment spending. This will increase planned aggregate expenditures and, as a result, output will rise and the recessionary gap will be reduce or eliminated. When the economy experiences inflationary pressures, the Fed may implement a contractionary monetary policy, or monetary tightening, by increasing interest rates with the intention of reducing an expansionary gap.

Learning Objective 9: Define and discuss the Fed's policy reaction function.
Economists often try to summarize the behavior of the Fed in terms of a **policy reaction function,** describing how the action a policymaker takes depends on the state of the economy. An example of a monetary policy reaction function is the Taylor rule, first proposed by John Taylor in 1993. The Taylor rule can be written as $r = 0.01 - 0.5 (Y^* - Y)/Y^* + 0.5\pi$, where r is the real interest rate, $(Y^* - Y)/Y^*$ is the output gap measured as a percentage of potential output, and π is and the rate of inflation. Thus, according to the Taylor rule, the Fed responds to both output gaps and the rate of inflation. It is important to understand, however, that the Taylor rule is not a legal restraint on the Fed. The Fed is perfectly free to deviate from it and does so when circumstances warrant. It is up to the Fed to determine its policy reaction function. Doing so is a complex process, involving a combination of statistical analysis of the economy and human judgment. In practice, monetary policymaking is as much an art as a science.

III. Self-Test

Key Terms
Match the term in the right-hand column with the appropriate definitions in the left-hand column by placing the letter of the term in the blank in front of its definition. (Answers are given at the end of the chapter.)

1. ____ The choice about which forms to hold one's wealth.   a. demand for money
2. ____ The interest rate that commercial banks charge each   b. federal funds rate
other for very short-term (usually overnight) loans.

3. ____ Shows the relationship between the aggregate quantity of money demanded and the nominal interest rate.

c. money demand curve

4. ____ Describes how the action a policymaker takes depends on the state of the economy.

d. policy reaction function

5. ____ The amount of wealth an individual chooses to hold in the form of money.

e. portfolio allocation decision

Multiple-Choice Questions
Circle the letter that corresponds to the best answer. (Answers are given at the end of the chapter.)

1. The portfolio allocation decision is related to the demand for money because
   A. money can be used to buy a portfolio.
   B. money is one of the many forms in which wealth can be held and is a part of most asset portfolios.
   C. the portfolio allocation decision determines how much of an individual's money is going to be held in the form of currency and how much in the form of balances in a checking account.
   D. money is the main form of wealth for most people.
   E. portfolio allocation explains why the amount of money people hold is directly related to interest rates.

2. E-Buy, a web-based auction firm receives an average of $25,000 in payments for its services each day, which it deposits in its bank account at the end of each day. E-Commerce Management Systems, Inc. proposed a computerized cash management system to track E-Buys' inflows and outflows of payments and electronically transfer the funds to an interest-bearing bank account. The cost of the system is $500 per year and E-Buys estimates that it would reduce its cash holding by approximately $10,000 per day. E-Buy should
   A. accept the proposal.
   B. reject the proposal.
   C. accept the proposal if the average interest rate they can earn on the funds is at least 10 percent.
   D. reject the proposal if the average interest rate they can earn on the funds is less than 10 percent.
   E. accept the proposal if the average interest rate they can earn on the funds is greater than 5 percent.

3. As the number of ATM machines increases in a country
   A. the supply of money will increase.
   B. the supply of money will decrease.
   C. people will hold more of their wealth in the form of money. (i.e., the demand for money will increase).
   D. people will hold less of their wealth in the form of money (i.e., the demand for money will decrease).
   E. interest rates will increase.

4. When the Fed buys government bonds, bond prices
    A. increase and interest rates fall.
    B. decrease and interest rates fall.
    C. increase and interest rates rise.
    D. decrease and interest rates rise.
    E. are unchanged and interest rates fall.

5. The Fed communicates its monetary policy to the public in terms of targets for the federal funds rate because it is
    A. the only interest rate that they can control.
    B. the interest rate that most individuals pay when they borrow money to buy a car, a household appliance, or a house.
    C. the interest rate that the Fed has the greatest control over.
    D. one of the tools of monetary policy.
    E. the most important of all the interest rates that are determined in the various financial markets.

6. The real interest rate
    A. cannot be controlled by the Fed because monetary policy only affects nominal interest rates.
    B. can be controlled by the Fed in the short run, but not in the long run.
    C. can be controlled by the Fed in the long run, but not in the short run.
    D. equals the nominal interest rate plus the inflation rate.
    E. equals the inflation rate minus the nominal interest rate.

7. If the Fed implements an open-market sale of government bonds, the
    A. money market equilibrium interest rate will rise.
    B. money market equilibrium interest rate will fall.
    C. price of bonds will rise.
    D. supply of money will increase.
    E. demand for bonds will decrease

8. If the Fed implements an open-market purchase of government bonds, this will cause a(n)
    A. decrease in consumption spending, an increase in investment spending, and an increase in planned aggregate expenditures.
    B. increase in consumption and investment spending and an increase in planned aggregate expenditures.
    C. decrease in consumption and investment spending and an increase in planned aggregate expenditures.
    D. decrease in consumption spending, a decrease in investment spending, and an increase in planned aggregate expenditures.
    E. increase in consumption spending, a decrease in investment spending, and a decrease in planned aggregate expenditures.

9. To close a recessionary gap the Fed should
   A. sell government bonds to increase bond prices and lower interest rates, causing consumption, investment spending, and planned aggregate expenditures to increase.
   B. sell government bonds to decrease bond prices and lower interest rates, causing consumption, investment spending, and planned aggregate expenditures to increase.
   C. buy government bonds to increase bond prices and lower interest rates, causing consumption, investment spending, and planned aggregate expenditures to increase.
   D. buy government bonds to decreases bond prices and increase interest rates, causing consumption, investment spending, and planned aggregate expenditures to decrease.
   E. buy government bonds to decreases bond prices and lower interest rates, causing consumption, investment spending, and planned aggregate expenditures to increase.

10. An expansionary monetary policy will cause a(n)
    A. decrease in interest rates, an increase in planned aggregate expenditures, and is designed to reduce an expansionary gap.
    B. increase in interest rates, a decrease in planned aggregate expenditures, and is designed to reduce an expansionary gap.
    C. decrease in interest rates, a decrease in planned aggregate expenditures, and is designed to reduce a recessionary gap.
    D. decrease in interest rates, an increase in planned aggregate expenditures, and is designed to reduce a recessionary gap.
    E. increase in interest rates, increase in planned aggregate expenditures, and is designed to reduce a recessionary gap.

11. The Fed's policy reaction function
    A. is mandated by the Taylor rule.
    B. is approximated by the Taylor rule.
    C. can be determined by statistical analysis of the economy.
    D. is determined by its short-run target rate of inflation.
    E. only provides information about the central bank's inflation target.

12. Monetary policymaking is based on
    A. scientific analyses, to apply detailed statistical modeling of the economy.
    B. the judgment of the members of the Federal Open Market Committee based on their experience as policymakers.
    C. a mathematical model of Taylor's rule.
    D. scientific analyses and art (i.e., the judgment of the members of the Federal Open-Market Committee).
    E. a mathematical model of Taylor's rule and art (i.e., the judgment of the members of the Federal Open-Market Committee).

13. The higher the price of bonds, with no change in the cost of transferring funds between bonds and checkable deposits, the
    A. more likely people are to hold their wealth in the form of bonds than money.
    B. more likely people are to hold their wealth in the form of money than bonds.
    C. the greater the differential between nominal and real interest rates.

    D. the smaller the quantity of money demanded.

    E. the greater the demand for money.

14. A decrease in aggregate real output or income will

    A. decrease the quantity of goods and services that people and businesses want to buy and sell and, thus, decrease the demand for money.

    B. decrease the quantity of goods and services that people and businesses want to buy and sell and, thus, increase the demand for money.

    C. increase the quantity of goods and services that people and businesses want to buy and sell and, thus, decrease the demand for money.

    D. increase the quantity of goods and services that people and businesses want to buy and sell and, thus, increase the demand for money.

    E. decrease the quantity of goods and services that people and businesses want to buy and sell, but have no effect on the demand for money.

15. A contractionary monetary policy

    A. is achieved if the Fed implements an open-market purchase of government bonds.

    B. will decrease the money market equilibrium interest rate.

    C. will increase the money market equilibrium interest rate.

    D. will raise the price of bonds.

    E. will shift the money supply curve to the right.

16. The Fed can control real interest rates only in the short run because

    A. the U.S. Congress has not given it legal authority to control interest rates in the long run.

    B. nominal interest rates only adjust slowly to changing economic conditions and policy.

    C. saving and investment are not relevant to short-run real interest rates.

    D. saving and investment are not relevant to long-run real interest rates.

    E. the inflation rate only adjusts slowly to changing economic conditions and policy.

17. If the Fed wants to lower the money market equilibrium interest rate, it should

    A. decrease the supply of money.

    B. shift the supply of money curve to the left.

    C. sell government bonds.

    D. purchase government bonds.

    E. decrease the price of bonds.

18. A contractionary monetary policy is designed to produce a(n)

    A. increase in planned aggregate expenditures and reduce an expansionary gap.

    B. decrease in planned aggregate expenditures and reduce an expansionary gap.

    C. increase in planned aggregate expenditures and reduce a recessionary gap.

    D. decrease in planned aggregate expenditures and reduce a recessionary gap.

    E. increase in planned aggregate expenditures and increase an expansionary gap.

19. If the Fed purchases government bonds, this will cause a(n)

    A. increase in planned aggregate expenditures and output and reduce a recessionary gap.

    B. increase in planned aggregate expenditures and output and reduce an expansionary gap.

C. decrease in planned aggregate expenditures and output and reduce a recessionary gap.
D. decrease in planned aggregate expenditures and output and reduce an expansionary gap.
E. increase in planned aggregate expenditures and decrease output and reduce an expansionary gap.

20. The "art" of monetary policymaking is necessary because
A. of Taylor's rule.
B. the Fed does not have precise information about the size of the money supply and the level of interest rates.
C. the Fed does not have precise information about the level of potential output and the size and speed of the effects of its actions.
D. the Fed does not have precise information about the level of actual output and the size and speed of the effects of its actions.
E. the Fed does not have precise information about the level of planned aggregate expenditures and the size and speed of the effects of its actions.

Short Answer Problems
(Answers and solutions are given at the end of the chapter.)

1. Cost and Benefit of Holding Money
The following table shows the estimated annual benefits to Siam of holding different amounts of money.

Average Money Holdings	Total Annual Benefit	Marginal Annual Benefit
$1,000	$60	XXXXXXXX
1,100	72	
1,200	82	
1,300	90	
1,400	96	
1,500	100	
1,600	102	
1,700	102	

A. Complete column 3 by calculating the extra benefit of each additional $100 in money holdings greater than $100.
B. How much money will Siam hold if the nominal interest rates is 10 percent? $_____; if the nominal interest rates is 8 percent? $_____; if the nominal interest rates is 6 percent? $_____; if the nominal interest rate is 4 percent $_____; if the nominal interest rate is 2 percent $_____?

C. On the graph below plot Siam's money demand curve for nominal interest rates between 2
   and 12 percent.

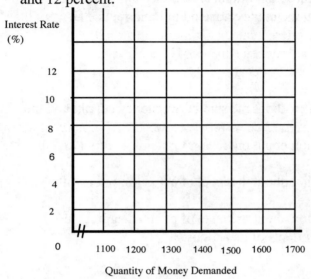

Quantity of Money Demanded

D. If Siam won a million-dollar lottery, his money demand curve shift to the (right/left)
   _____ representing a(n) (increase/decrease) _____ in the demand for
   money.

2. Money Market and Equilibrium Interest Rate

This problem focuses on the Fed's control of the money supply to achieve targeted nominal
interest rates. Assume that the price level and real GDP are at levels such that the money demand
is initially at MD₁.

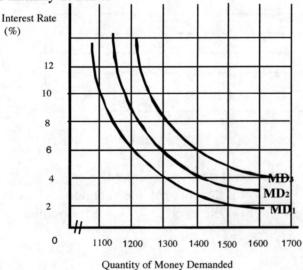

Quantity of Money Demanded

A. If the Fed wants to set the nominal equilibrium interest rate at 4 percent, it should set the
   money supply at $ _____.
B. If real GDP increases so that the money demand rises to MD₂ and the Fed wants to keep the
   nominal equilibrium interest rate at 4 percent, it should (increase/decrease) _____ the
   nominal money supply to $ _____.

C. If the Fed now decides to raise the nominal equilibrium interest rate to 6 percent, it should (increase/decrease) _____ the nominal money supply to $ _____.

D. If the price level subsequently rises causing the money demand to increase to MD_3 and the Fed wants to keep the nominal equilibrium interest rate at 6 percent, it should (increase/decrease) _____ the nominal money supply to $_____.

3. Monetary Policy and Short-Run Equilibrium Output

This problem will help you to better understand the relationship between interest rates, planned aggregate expenditures, output, and monetary policy. The planned aggregate expenditures for the economy of Hinderland is given by the following equations:

$C = \$750 + 0.75(Y - T) - 300r$

$I^P = \$400 - 600r$

$G = \$500$

$T = \$400$

$NX = -\$55$

A. If the Fed sets the nominal interest rate (r) at 0.05 (5%), the planned aggregate expenditures for the Hinderland economy would be represented by the equation $PAE = \$$_____ + .75Y.

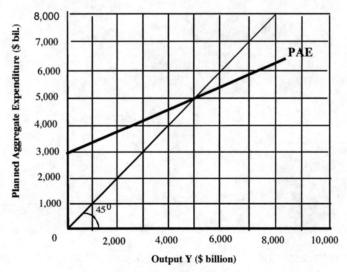

B. Given the Hinderland planned aggregate expenditures in the above graph, the short-run equilibrium output would equal $_____ .

C. If potential output (Y^*) in the Hinderland economy equals $5,050, there would be a(n) _____ gap of $_____ .

D. If the Fed wanted to close the output gap, it should implement a(n) (expansionary/ contractionary) _____ monetary policy.

Note: Questions 3E – 3F require an algebraic solution using the PAE equation from question 3A. The use of algebraic equations to determine monetary policy is discussed in Appendix A of the textbook chapter.

E. To close the gap, the Fed would need to (decrease/ increase) _____ nominal interest rates to _____ percent.

F. Following the expansionary monetary policy, assume the recessionary gap is closed at $Y =$ $5,050 and the Fed determines that the inflation rate is 1.5%. Applying the Taylor rule, this would suggest that the real interest rate in the economy would equal_____ %.

IV. Economic Naturalist Application

In Economic Naturalist 14.4, the Fed's role in responding to the recession that began in the fall of 2000 and the terrorist attacks of September 11, 2001, are discussed. It concludes by stating, "As of this writing, a (weak) recovery from the recession that began in 2001 appears to be under way." Assuming the recovery continues and eventually strengthens, what type of monetary policy is likely to be implemented? If the recovery fails to strengthen and the economy falls back into recession, how is the Fed likely to respond?

V. Go To the Web: Graphing Exercises Using Interactive Graphs

How Can the Federal Reserve Reduce the Threat of Inflation?

During 1999 and early 2000, consumer spending was increasing faster than the productive capacity of the economy, creating an expansionary gap that pushed the unemployment rate to its lowest level in 30 years but also increased the threat of inflation. According to the basic Keynesian model, what should the Federal Reserve do in this situation to reduce the possibility of future inflation and return the economy to its potential output level?
Answer:

To review an answer to this question, and to learn more about the use of economic theory to analyze this issue (and other macroeconomic issues), please go to the Electronic Learning Session in the Student Center at the Frank/Bernanke web site: http://www.mhhe.com/economics/frankbernanke2.

VI. Self-Test Solutions

Key Terms
1. e
2. b
3. c
4. d
5. a

Multiple-Choice Questions
1. B
2. E $10,000 x 0.05 = $500. Therefore, an interest rate of greater than 5% would imply that the benefit would be greater than the cost.
3. D
4. A
5. C
6. B
7. A
8. B
9. C
10. D
11. B
12. C
13. B
14. A
15. C
16. E
17. D
18. B
19. A
20. C

Short Answer Problems
1.
A.

Average Money Holdings	Total Annual Benefit	Marginal Annual Benefit
$1,000	$60	XXXXXXXX
1,100	72	12
1,200	82	10
1,300	90	8
1,400	97	7
1,500	103	6
1,600	107	4
1,700	109	2

B. $1,200; $1,300; $1,500; $1,600; $1,700

C.

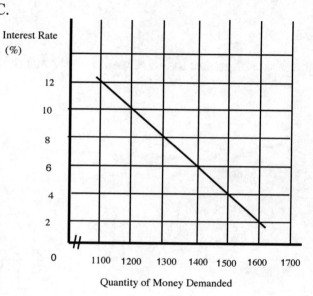

Interest Rate (%) vs. Quantity of Money Demanded

D. right; increase

2.
A. $1300
B. increase; $1,400
C. decrease; $1,300
D. increase; $1,400

3.
A. $1,250 ($750 + .75(Y − $300) − $300(.05) + $400 − $600(.05) + $500 + (−$55)
B. $5,000
C. recessionary gap; $50 (Y* − Y = output gap)
D. expansionary
E. decrease; 3.6 ($5,050 = $1,295 + .75($5,050) − 900i, or $5,050 = $1,295 + $3,787.5 − 900$i$.
  Combining the constant values gives us −$32.5 = − 900$i$, or 3.6 = i)
F. 1.75 [r = 0.01 − 0.5 ($\frac{\$5,050 - \$5,050}{\$5,050}$) + 0.5(.015)]

Chapter 17
Exchange Rates and the Open Economy

I. Pretest: What Do You Really Know?
Circle the letter that corresponds to the best answer. (Answers appear immediately after the final question).

1. The nominal exchange rate is the
   A. market on which currencies of various nations are traded for one another.
   B. price of the average domestic good or service relative to the price of the average foreign good or service, when prices are expressed in terms of a common currency.
   C. quantity of foreign currency held by a government for the purpose of purchasing the domestic currency in the foreign exchange market.
   D. rate at which two currencies can be traded for each other.
   E. rate at which a good in one country can be traded for the same good in another country.

2. The following table provides the nominal exchange rates for the U.S. dollar:

Country	Foreign currency/dollar	Dollar/foreign currency
Saudi Arabia (riyal)	6.167	.162
Brazil (real)	1.850	.541

   Based on these data, the nominal exchange rate equals _____ Brazilian reals per Saudi riyal or equivalently _____ Saudi riyals per Brazilian real.
   A. 1.053; .95
   B. .95; 1.053
   C. .30; 3.33
   D. 3.33; .30
   E. 6.490; .154

3. An exchange rate that varies according to the supply and demand for the currency in the foreign exchange market is called a(n) _____ exchange rate.
   A. overvalued
   B. undervalued
   C. fixed
   D. flexible
   E. real

4. The real exchange rate is the
   A. market in which currencies of various nations are traded for one another.
   B. price of the average domestic good or service relative to the price of the average foreign good or service, when prices are expressed in terms of a common currency.
   C. quantity of foreign currency held by a government for the purpose of purchasing domestic currency in the foreign exchange market.
   D. rate at which two currencies can be traded for each other.
   E. rate at which a good in one country can be traded for the same good in another country.

5. Net exports will tend to be high when the real exchange rate
   A. is high.
   B. is low.
   C. equals the nominal exchange rate.
   D. appreciates.
   E. is strong.

6. If a certain automotive part can be purchased in Mexico for 45 pesos or in the United States for $6.25 and if the nominal exchange rate is 9 pesos per U.S. dollar, then the real exchange rate for automotive part equals
   A. 1.25
   B. 51.20
   C. .125
   D. 0.8
   E. 8

7. The theory that nominal exchange rates are determined as necessary for the law of one price to hold is called
   A. the fixed-exchange-rate rule.
   B. the equilibrium principle.
   C. the law of supply and demand.
   D. purchasing power parity.
   E. international equality.

8. The price of gold is $300 per ounce in New York and 2,850 pesos per ounce in Mexico City. If the law of one price holds for gold, the nominal exchange rate is _____ pesos per U.S. dollar.
   A. .105
   B. 1.053
   C. 9.5
   D. 95.5
   E. 25

9. The purchasing power parity theory is not a good explanation of nominal exchange rate determination in the short run because
   A. there is no evidence that low inflation is association with less rapid nominal exchange rate depreciation.

B. there is no evidence that high inflation is associated with more rapid nominal exchange rate depreciation.

C. most goods and services are traded internationally and are standardized.

D. many goods and services are nontraded and not all traded goods are standardized.

E. most nominal exchange rates are fixed and foreign exchange markets do not bring the supply and demand for currencies into equilibrium.

10. The U.S. dollar exchange rate, e, where e is the nominal exchange rate expressed as Japanese yen per U.S. dollar, will appreciate when

A. real GDP in the U.S. increases.

B. real GDP in Japan decreases.

C. the U.S. Federal Reserve tightens monetary policy.

D. U.S. consumers increase their preference for Japanese cars.

E. the Bank of Japan tightens monetary policy.

Solutions and Feedback to Pretest

For each question you incorrectly answered, we strongly recommend taking the time to review the appropriate material before continuing. In the table below, the relevant textbook pages are listed for each question as well as the pertinent Learning Objective from the following Key Point Review.

Correct Answer	Textbook Page Numbers	Learning Objective
1. D	pp. 470-72	1
2. C	pp. 470-72	1
3. D	p. 473	1
4. B	pp. 473-76	2
5. B	p. 476	2
6. A	p. 475	2
7. D	p. 477	3
8. C	p. 478	3
9. D	pp. 478-80	3
10. C	pp. 480-83	4

II. Key Point Review

This chapter explains the role of exchange rates in open economies. The discussion begins by distinguishing between the nominal exchange rate and the real exchange rate. This is followed by an analysis of how flexible and fixed exchange rates are determined. The chapter concludes with a discussion of the relative merits of fixed and flexible exchange rates.

Learning Objective 1: Define nominal exchange rate, appreciation, and depreciation.

The economic benefits of trade between nations in goods, services, and assets are similar to the benefits of trade within a nation. There is, however, a difference between the two cases. Trade within a nation normally involves only a single currency, while trade between nations involves different currencies. Because international transactions generally require that one currency be traded for another currency, the relative values of different currencies are an important factor in international economic relations. The rate at which two currencies can be traded for each other is called the **nominal exchange rate**, or simply the exchange rate. Exchange rates can be expressed as the amount of foreign currency needed to purchase one unit of domestic currency, or as the number of units of the domestic currency needed to purchase one unit of the foreign currency. These two ways of expressing the exchange rate are equivalent; each is the reciprocal of the other. Although the exchange rate can be expressed either way, to simply the discussion, the textbook authors have chosen to define the nominal exchange rate (*e*) as the number of units of foreign currency that domestic currency will buy. Exchange rates can be of two broad types flexible or fixed exchange rates. A **flexible exchange rate** is not officially fixed, but varies according to the supply and demand for the currency in the **foreign exchange market**–the market in which currencies of various nations are traded for one another. Flexible exchange rates change over time. An increase in the value of one currency relative to other currencies is called **appreciation,** and a decrease in the value of that currency relative to other currencies is called **depreciation.** A **fixed exchange rate** is an exchange rate whose value is set by official government policy.

Hint: Since the exchange rates of any two currencies are the reciprocal of each other, if you know the exchange rate of a U.S. dollar in terms of Mexican pesos you can easily determine the exchange of a Mexican peso in terms of U.S. dollars. For example, if $1 exchanges for 10 Mexican pesos, then simply divide $1 by 10 to determine how many dollars you would get for one Mexican peso (i.e., 1 divided by 10 equals $.10 per Mexican peso.

Learning Objective 2: Define real exchange rates, and explain the economic importance of the real exchange rate.

It is important to distinguish the nominal exchange rate from the real exchange rate. As indicated above, the nominal exchange rate tells us the price of the domestic currency in terms of a foreign currency. The **real exchange rate** tells us the price of the average domestic good or service in terms of the average foreign good or service, when prices are expressed in terms of a common currency. The real exchange rate is equal to the nominal exchange rate times the price of the average domestic good divided by the price of the average foreign good. Consequently, the nominal and real exchange rates tend to move in the same direction. The real exchange rate has important implications for a nation's trade. A high real exchange rate implies that domestic producers will have a hard time exporting to other countries, while foreign goods will sell well in the home country. Thus, when the real exchange rate is high, net exports will tend to be low. Conversely, if the real exchange rate is low, domestic producers will find it easier to export and foreign producers will have difficulty selling in the domestic market. Net exports, therefore, will be high when the real exchange rate is low. This cause-and-effect relationship suggests that a strong currency does not necessarily reflect a strong economy.

Learning Objective 3: Define the law of one price and purchasing power parity (PPP), and explain the PPP theory of exchange rate determination, its implications and shortcomings.
What determines the value of flexible exchanges rates? The most basic theory of how nominal exchange rates are determined is called **purchasing power parity**, or PPP. To understand the PPP theory, one first has to understand the law of one price. The **law of one price** states that if transportation costs are relatively small, the price of an internationally traded commodity must be the same in all locations. If the law of one price were to hold for all goods and services, then the value of the exchange rate between two currencies would be determined by dividing the price of the average good in one country by the price of the average good in the other country. An implication of the PPP theory is that, in the long run, the currencies of countries that experience significant inflation will tend to depreciate. The rationale is sound because inflation implies that a nation's currency is losing purchasing power in the domestic market, while exchange-rate depreciation implies that the nation's currency is losing purchasing power in international markets.

> **Note:** The law of one price is an application of the equilibrium principle. According to the equilibrium principle, the international market for a commodity (e.g., a currency) would return to equilibrium only when all unexploited opportunities for profit had been eliminated (i.e., when the price is the same in all locations).

Empirical studies have found that the PPP theory is useful for predicting changes in nominal exchange rates over the long run. The theory is less successful, however, in predicting short-run movements in exchange rates. One reason that the PPP works less well in the short run is that the law of one price works best for standardized commodities that are widely traded. Not all goods, however, are standardized commodities and not all goods are traded internationally. In general, the greater the share of traded and standardized goods and services in a nation's output, the more precisely the PPP theory will apply to the country's exchange rate.

Learning Objective 4: Use supply-and-demand analysis to determine the short-run movements in flexible exchange rates.
Supply and demand analysis is more useful for understanding the short-run movements of exchange rates. Anyone who holds a currency is a potential supplier of that currency, but, in practice, the principal suppliers of a currency to the foreign exchange market are that nation's households and firms. The demanders of a currency are, in practice, households and firms that want to purchase foreign assets or goods and services. The supply curve of a currency is upward sloping and the demand curve is downward sloping. The equilibrium value of a currency, also

called the **fundamental value of the exchange rate**, is the exchange rate at which the quantity supplied equals the quantity demanded. Factors that cause shifts in the supply and demand for a currency will cause the equilibrium value of the currency to change. Some factors that cause an increase in the supply of the domestic currency are an increased preference for foreign goods, an increase in the domestic real GDP, and an increase in the real interest rate on foreign assets.

Factors that cause an increased demand for the domestic currency include an increased preference for domestic goods, an increase in real GDP abroad, and an increase in the real interest rate on domestic assets. Of the many factors affecting a country's exchange rate, among the most important is the monetary policy of a country's central bank. A tightening of a country's monetary policy increases domestic real interest rates, raising the demand for its currency and causing the currency to appreciate. Easing of monetary policy has the opposite effects. In an open economy with a flexible exchange rate, the exchange rate serves as another channel for monetary policy that reinforces the effects of real interest rates. Higher interest rates, for example, reduce domestic consumption and investment. They also cause appreciation of the currency and, as a result, imports rise and exports fall, reducing net exports. The decline in net exports, thus, reinforces the domestic effects of the tightened monetary policy. Monetary policy, therefore, is more effective in an open economy with flexible exchange rates.

Learning Objective 5: Define fixed exchange rates, devaluation and revaluation.
Fixed exchange rates historically have been an important alternative to flexible exchange rates. Fixed exchange rates are still used in many countries, especially small and developing nations. A **fixed exchange rate** is an exchange rate whose value is is set by official government policy (in practice, usually the by the finance ministry or treasury department, in cooperation with the country's central bank). Fixed exchange rates today are usually set in terms of a major currency (e.g., the dollar or yen), or relative to a "basket" of currencies, typically those of the country's trading partners. Historically, currency values were fixed in terms of gold or other precious metals. Once an exchange rate has been fixed, the government usually attempts to keep it unchanged for some time. Economic circumstances, however, can force the government to change the value of the exchange rate. A reduction in the official value of a currency is called **devaluation**; and increase in the official value is called a **revaluation**.

Learning Objective 6: Explain the fundamental value of the exchange rate and the implications of an overvalued or undervalued currency.
Fixed exchange rates are not always consistent with the fundamental value of a currency (as determined by supply and demand). When the officially fixed value of an exchange rate is greater than its fundamental value, the exchange rate is **overvalued**, and when it is less that its fundamental value, it is **undervalued**. When the officially set value of an exchange rate is overvalued, the government has several alternatives for dealing with the inconsistency. It could devalue its currency, restrict international transactions, or become a demander of its currency. The most common approach is for the government to become a demander of its currency. To be able to purchase its own currency and maintain an overvalued exchange rate, a government (usually the central bank) must hold foreign-currency assets called **international reserves**, or simply reserves. Because a government must use part of its reserves to maintain an overvalued currency, over time its reserves will decline. The net decline in a country's stock of international reserves over a year is called its **balance-of-payments deficit**. Conversely, if a country

experiences a net increase in its international reserves over a year, it has a **balance-of-payments surplus**. Although a government can maintain an overvalued exchange rate for some time by purchasing its own currency, there is a limit to this strategy because no government's reserves are unlimited. Eventually a government will run out of reserves, and the fixed exchange rate will collapse. A **speculative attack**, involving massive selling of domestic-currency assets by financial investors, can quickly end a government's attempt to maintain an overvalued currency. Such an attack is most likely to occur when financial investors fear that an overvalued currency will be devalued. A speculative attack, therefore, can be self-fulfilling.

Note: Speculative attacks on currencies are not uncommon, especially in recent years as more countries have opened their economies to foreign investment. For example, see Economic Naturalist 17.4 that explains the causes and consequences of the Asian crisis of 1997-98.

As an alternative to trying to maintain an overvalued currency, a government can take actions to try to increase the fundamental value of its currency and eliminate the overvaluation problem. The most effective way to increase the fundamental value of a currency is through monetary policy. A tightening of monetary policy that raises real interest rates will increase the demand for a currency and, in turn, will raise its fundamental value. Although monetary policy can be used in this manner, it has some drawbacks. In particular, if monetary policy is used to set the fundamental value of the exchange rate equal to the official value, it is no longer available for stabilizing the domestic economy. The conflict between using monetary policy to set the fundamental value of a currency or using it to stabilize the domestic economy is most severe when the exchange rate is under a speculative attack.

Learning Objective 7: Compare fixed and flexible exchange rate systems.
There are two important issues in comparing flexible and fixed exchange rates – the effects on monetary policy and the effects on trade and economic integration. A flexible exchange rate strengthens the impact of monetary policy on aggregate demand, when a fixed exchange rate prevents policymakers from using monetary policy to stabilize the domestic economy. Large economies should almost always employ flexible exchange rates because it seldom makes sense for them to give up the power to stabilize the domestic economy via monetary policy. For small economies, however, giving up this power may make sense when their history suggests an inability to use monetary policy to control domestic inflation. On the issue of trade and economic integration, supporters of fixed exchange rates have argued that an officially fixed exchange rate reduces or eliminates uncertainty about future exchange rates and, thus, provides incentives for firms to expand export business. The problem with this argument is that a fixed exchange rate is not guaranteed to remain fixed forever, especially if the currency comes under a speculative attack. Some countries, such as eleven Western European nations, have tried to solve the problem of uncertain exchange rates by adopting a common currency.

III. Self-Test

Key Terms
Match the term in the right-hand column with the appropriate definitions in the left-hand column by placing the letter of the term in the blank in front of its definition. (Answers are given at the end of the chapter.)

1. _____ The exchange rate that equates the quantities of the currency supplied and demanded in the foreign exchange market.	a. appreciation
2. _____ An exchange rate that has an officially fixed value greater than its fundamental value.	b. balance-of-payments deficit
3. _____ The price of the average domestic good or service relative to the price of the average foreign good or service, when prices are expressed in terms of a common currency.	c. balance-of-payments surplus
4. _____ A massive selling of domestic currency assets by financial investors.	d. depreciation
5. _____ A reduction in the official value of a currency (in a fixed-exchange-rate system).	e. devaluation
6. _____ If transportation costs are relatively small, the price of an internationally traded commodity must be the same in all locations.	f. fixed exchange rate
7. _____ An exchange rate whose value is not officially fixed but varies according to the supply and demand for the currency in the foreign exchange market.	g. flexible exchange rate
8. _____ The rate at which two currencies can be traded for each other.	h. foreign-exchange market
9. _____ Foreign currency assets held by a government for the purpose of purchasing the domestic currency in the foreign exchange market.	i. fundamental value of the exchange rate
10. _____ An exchange rate whose value is set by official government policy.	j. international reserves
11. _____ The net increase in a country's stock of international reserves over a year.	k. law of one price
12. _____ An exchange rate that has an officially fixed value less than its fundamental value.	l. nominal exchange rate
13. _____ An increase in the value of a currency relative to other currencies.	m. overvalued exchange rate
14. _____ The market on which currencies from various nations are traded for one another.	n. purchasing power parity (PPP)
15. _____ An increase in the official value of a currency (in a fixed-exchange-rate system).	o. real exchange rate
16. _____ The theory that nominal exchange rates are determined as necessary for the law of one price to hold.	p. revaluation
17. _____ The net decline in a country's stock of international reserves over a year.	q. speculative attack

18.____ A decrease in the value of a currency relative to other   r.   undervalued
currencies.   exchange rate

Multiple-Choice Questions
Circle the letter that corresponds to the best answer. (Answers are given at the end of the chapter.)

1. During summer 2000, the nominal exchange rate was one U.S. dollar to 9.5 Mexican pesos. The dollar per peso equivalent exchange rate equaled
   A. 9.5 dollars per peso.
   B. .095 dollars per peso.
   C. 10.5 dollars per peso.
   D. .105 dollars per peso.
   E. 105 dollars per peso.

2. A disposable camera cost $8 in the United States and 110 pesos in Mexico during the summer of 2000. The exchange rate at that time was 9.5 pesos per dollar. The real exchange rate of the dollar (for disposable cameras) equaled
   A. 9.5.
   B. .69.
   C. .84.
   D. 92.6.
   E. .105.

3. During the 1980s, the United States had a balance-of-payments deficit with South Korea and Taiwan. The U.S. government complained that the governments of those two nations were manipulating their exchange rates to promote exports to the United States. Apparently, the White House believed that the
   A. currencies of South Korea and Taiwan were overvalued relative to the dollar.
   B. currencies of South Korea and Taiwan were undervalued relative to the dollar.
   C. South Korean currency was overvalued relative to the currency of Taiwan.
   D. South Korean currency was undervalued relative to the currency of Taiwan.
   E. dollar should be allowed to appreciate against the currencies of South Korea and Taiwan.

4. Between 1973 and 1999, annual inflation in developing nations that export mainly manufactured goods averaged 23 percent, while inflation averaged 59 percent in countries that mainly export raw materials. Other things equal, the PPP theory would predict that, in the long run, the currencies of the raw materials exporting countries should have
   A. been approximately stable relative to the currencies of countries exporting manufactured goods.
   B. appreciated relative to the currencies of countries exporting manufactured goods.
   C. depreciated relative to the currencies of countries exporting manufactured goods.
   D. had no predictable relationship to the currencies of countries exporting manufactured goods.
   E. been perfectly stable relative to the currencies of countries exporting manufactured goods because they maintained fixed exchange rates.

5. The PPP theory works better in the long run than it does in the short run because
   A. the law of one price only pertains to the long run.
   B. not all goods and services are traded internationally, and not all goods are heterogeneous commodities.
   C. all goods and services are traded internationally, and not all goods are heterogeneous commodities.
   D. not all goods and services are traded internationally, and not all goods are standardized commodities.
   E. all goods and services are traded internationally, and all goods are standardized commodities.

6. In the early 1980s, high interest rates in the United States attracted enormous amounts of capital into the United States to buy stocks, bonds, real estate, and other assets. All other things equal, supply-and-demand analysis of exchange rates would predict that the U.S. dollar would experience _____ relative to other currencies.
   A. depreciation
   B. appreciation
   C. devaluation
   D. revaluation
   E. purchasing price parity

7. During 1999 and 2000, the U.S. Federal Reserve Bank tightened its monetary policy and interest rates in the United States increased in order to reduce domestic consumption and investment spending. In the short run, one would predict a(n)
   A. depreciation of the dollar and an increase in net exports.
   B. depreciation of the dollar and a decrease in net exports.
   C. devaluation of the dollar and a decrease in net exports.
   D. appreciation of the dollar and an increase in net exports.
   E. appreciation of the dollar and a decrease in net exports.

8. The value of a fixed exchange rate in contemporary economies is
   A. determined by the supply and demand for a currency in the foreign exchange market.
   B. set by the government, usually in terms of gold or some other precious metal.
   C. set by the government, usually in terms of the currency (or basket of currencies) of the country's major trading partner(s).
   D. set by agreement of the central banks of the major trading countries of the world.
   E. determined by economic forces.

9. During the 1990s, the government of Malaysia fixed the exchange rate of the Baht to the dollar. During the spring of 1998, investors perceived that the Baht was overvalued and a speculative attack ensued. What alternatives did the Malaysian government have to deal with this problem?
   A. It could have revalued the Baht, limited international transactions, purchased Baht on the foreign exchange market, or tightened domestic monetary policy.

B. It could have devalued the Baht, limited international transactions, purchased Baht on the foreign exchange market, or tightened domestic monetary policy.

C. It could have devalued the Baht, limited international transactions, sold Baht on the foreign exchange market, or tightened domestic monetary policy.

D. It could have revalued the Baht, limited international transactions, sold Baht on the foreign exchange market, or eased domestic monetary policy.

E. It could have revalued the Baht, limited international transactions, sold Baht on the foreign exchange market, or tightened domestic monetary policy.

10. During the 1930s, the United States was on the gold standard, creating a system of fixed exchange rates between the dollar and other currencies whose values were also set in terms of gold. As a result, monetary policy

A. could not be used to stabilize the U.S. economy during the Great Depression.

B. could be used to stabilize the U.S. economy during the Great Depression.

C. was immune to a speculative attack because devaluation was not possible.

D. was eased to counteract the banking panic and the bank failures during the Great Depression.

E. was used to decrease interest rates to counteract the economic decline brought on by the bank failures during the Great Depression.

11. When the real exchange rate of a country's currency is low, the home country will

A. find it easier to import, while domestic producers will have difficulty exporting.

B. find it easier to export, while domestic residents will buy more imports.

C. find it harder to export, while domestic residents will buy fewer imports.

D. find it easier to export, while domestic residents will buy fewer imports.

E. find it harder to export, while domestic residents will buy more imports.

12. Between 1990 and 1999, inflation in the United States averaged 2-3% per year, while Mexico experienced double-digit average annual inflation rates. Since the Mexican government did not try to maintain a fixed exchange rate, the PPP theory would suggest that, in the long run, the Mexican peso would

A. appreciate against the dollar and Mexico's net exports to the United States decreased.

B. appreciate against the dollar and Mexico's net exports to the United States increased.

C. depreciate against the dollar and Mexico's net exports to the United States increased.

D. depreciate against the dollar and Mexico's net exports to the United States decreased.

E. remain stable relative to the dollar, with no change in Mexico's net exports to the United States.

13. The PPP theory would be most useful in predicting

A. short-run changes in the exchange rate for a country that mainly produces heavily traded, standardized goods.

B. long-run changes in the exchange rate for a country that mainly produces heavily traded, standardized goods.

C. short-run changes in the exchange rate for a country that mainly produces lightly traded, standardized goods.

    D. long-run changes in the exchange rate for a country that mainly produces lightly traded, nonstandardized goods.

    E. short-run changes in the exchange rate for a country that mainly produces lightly traded, standardized goods.

14. The fundamental value of a country's exchange rate is
    A. constant over a prolonged period of time.
    B. determined by the supply of the country's currency in the foreign exchange market.
    C. determined by the demand for the country's currency in the foreign exchange market.
    D. determined by the supply of and demand for the country's currency in the domestic financial market.
    E. determined by the supply of and demand for the country's currency in the foreign exchange market.

15. During the latter half of the 1990s, real GDP in the United States grew faster than in most other industrial countries. All other things equal, supply-and-demand analysis of exchange rates would predict that, in the short run, the U.S. dollar would _____ relative to the currencies of the other industrialized countries.
    A. appreciate
    B. depreciate
    C. devaluate
    D. revaluate
    E. remain constant

16. If the central bank of England were to respond to a slowdown in the domestic economy by easing monetary policy, all other things equal, one would predict in the short run a(n)
    A. increase in the real interest rate, an increase in demand for the pound, and an appreciation in the pound.
    B. decrease in the real interest rate, an increase in demand for the pound, and an appreciation in the pound.
    C. decrease in the real interest rate, a decrease in demand for the pound, and a depreciation in the pound.
    D. increase in the real interest rate, a decrease in demand for the pound, and a depreciation in the pound.
    E. increase in the real interest rate, an increase in demand for the pound, and a depeciation in the pound.

17. If a country fixes the exchange rate for its currency relative to other currencies, and if the official exchange rate is overvalued relative to its fundamental value, then
    A. the most likely ultimate outcome is a depreciation of its currency.
    B. the most likely ultimate outcome is a devaluation of its currency.
    C. the most likely ultimate outcome is a revaluation of its currency.
    D. it will likely be able to indefinitely support its value by using its international reserves to buy its currency on the foreign exchange market.
    E. it can ease its monetary policy to increase the fundamental value of its currency and eliminate the overvalued status.

18. If exchange rates are flexible, a surplus in a nation's balance of payments would imply that the
    A. government will have to devalue the nation's currency.
    B. government will have to revalue the nation's currency.
    C. nation's exchange rate will remain unchanged.
    D. nation's exchange rate will appreciate.
    E. nation's exchange rate will depreciate.

19. Other things being equal, a recession in the United States combined with rapid economic growth in Japan would be expected to cause
    A. the dollar to appreciate against the yen.
    B. the dollar to depreciate against the yen.
    C. the yen to appreciate against the dollar.
    D. no predictable change in the dollar-yen exchange rate.
    E. Japan's demand curve for dollars to shift to the left.

20. In comparison to a fixed exchange rate system, a flexible exchange rate system
    A. weakens the impact of monetary policy on aggregate demand.
    B. strengthens the impact of monetary policy on aggregate demand.
    C. increases uncertainty about the future exchange rate.
    D. decreases uncertainty about the future exchange rate.
    E. is more likely to suffer from speculative attacks.

Short Answer Problems
(Answers and solutions are given at the end of the chapter.)

1. Nominal Exchange Rates
In this problem you can practice calculating the nominal exchange rates of currencies in terms of the amount of foreign currency needed to purchase one dollar and the number of dollars needed to purchase one unit of the foreign currency.

Nominal Exchange Rate for the U.S. Dollar (June 29, 2000)

Country	Foreign currency / dollar	Dollar / foreign currency
Britain (Pound)		1.5193
Canada (Dollar		.6742
Europe (Euro)		.95250
Germany (Mark)	2.054	
Japan (Yen)	105.06	
Mexico (Peso)	9.91	

Source: *Investor's Business Daily*, June 30, 2000 p. A22.

A. Based on the number of dollars needed to purchase one unit of the foreign currency, calculate the amount of foreign currency needed to purchase one dollar for the British pound, Canadian dollar, and the European euro in Column 2 of the above table.

B. Based on the amount of foreign currency needed to purchase one dollar, calculate the number of dollars needed to purchase one unit of the foreign currency for the German mark, Japanese yen, and Mexican peso in Column 3 of the above table.

C. During June, 2000, in the Monterrey, Mexico, newspaper, *El Norte*, a popular American/ German make of automobile was advertised at the price of 152,100 pesos. During the same time, it was advertised in the *Austin American Statesman* newspaper for 18,995 dollars. Based on the above peso–dollar exchange rate and the advertised prices for the automobile, the real exchange rate (for the automobile) equaled _____ (round your answer to the nearest hundredth).

D. The real exchange rate for the automobile implies that the price of the U.S. automobile is (more/less) _____ expensive than the Mexican automobile, putting the (U.S./Mexican) _____ product at a disadvantage.

2. Supply and Demand Analysis of the Exchange Rate

Supply and demand analysis is applied to the determination of the exchange rate in this problem. You will determine the equilibrium exchange rate and analyze the effects of changes in various factors on the supply of or demand for dollars to determine the impact on the equilibrium exchange rate. Answer the questions below based on the following graph illustrating the supply and demand for dollars in the euro/dollar market.

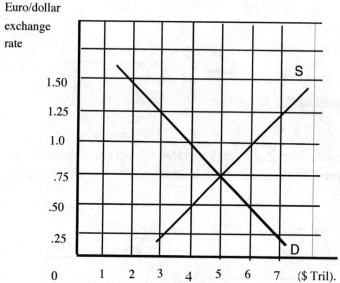

A. The equilibrium exchange rate of the dollar equals _____ euro(s) per dollar.

B. If European consumers' and businesses' preferences for American goods increases, the (supply/demand) _____ for dollars in the foreign exchange market will (increase/ decrease) _____ and the euro/dollar exchange will (increase/decrease) _____.

C. If the U.S. GDP increases, the (supply/demand) _____ for dollars in the foreign exchange market will (increase/decrease) _____ and the euro/dollar exchange will (increase/decrease) _____.

D. An increase in the real interest rate of European assets will (increase/decrease) _____ the (supply/demand) _____ of (for) dollars in the foreign exchange market and the euro/dollar exchange will (increase/decrease) _____.

E. If the Fed tightens U.S. monetary policy, the (supply/demand) _____ for dollars in the foreign exchange market will (increase/decrease) _____ and the euro/dollar exchange rate will (increase/decrease) _____ .

3. Fundamental Value of a Currency and the Balance of Payments Deficit

The demand and supply for Surican pesos in the foreign exchange market are given by the following equations (e is the Surican exchange rate measured in dollars per Surican peso).
Demand = 55,000 – 88,000 e
Supply = 25,000 + 32,000 e

A. The fundamental value of the Surican peso (e) equals _____ .
B. If the Surican government set the official exchange rate at .333 dollars per peso, the demand for Surican pesos would equal _____, and the supply of Surican pesos would be

_____ .
C. The quantity supplied of Surican pesos would be (greater than/less than/equal to) _____ the quantity demanded for Surican pesos.
D. To maintain the fixed exchange rate, the Surican government would have to purchase _____ Surican pesos. Since the Surican peso is purchased at the official rate of 3 pesos to the dollar, the balance of payments deficit in dollars would equal $_____ .

IV. Economic Naturalist Application

In Economic Naturalist 17.1, the authors explain why a strong U.S. dollar does not necessarily imply a strong U.S. economy. For example, it compares the exchange rate of the U.S. dollar during 1973, when the dollar was worth more in terms of other major currencies and the economy was weak, and 2000 when the dollar was lower but the economy was stronger. Go to http://research.stlouisfed.org/fred/data/exchange.html to find the latest data on the U.S. dollar exchange rate and determine whether the dollar is stronger or weaker than it was in 2000. Discuss the implications of the change in the exchange on the current U.S. economy.
Answer:

V. Go to the Web: Graphing Exercises Using Interactive Graphs

Why Did the Dollar Appreciate against the Yen in the mid-1990s?

Between 1995 and 1998 the dollar appreciated from 85 yen per dollar to more than 140 yen per dollar. What were the economic reasons behind such a large increase in the yen-dollar exchange rate and what were the likely effects on the U.S. economy during this time?
Answer:

To learn more about the use of economic theory to analyze this issue (and other macroeconomic issues), please go to the Electronic Learning Session in the Student Center at the Frank/Bernanke web site: http://www.mhhe.com/economics/frankbernanke2.

VI. Self-Test Solutions

Key Terms

1. i
2. m
3. o
4. q
5. e
6. k
7. g
8. l
9. j
10. f
11. c
12. r
13. a
14. h
15. p
16. n
17. b
18. d

Multiple-Choice Questions

1. D (= 1/9.5)
2. B (= [9.5*8] / 110)
3. A
4. C
5. D
6. B
7. E
8. C
9. B
10. A
11. D
12. C
13. B
14. E
15. A
16. C
17. B
18. D
19. A
20. B

Short Answer Problems

1.
A., B.

Country	Foreign currency / dollar	Dollar / foreign currency
Britain (Pound)	.6582 (= 1/1.5193)	1.5193
Canada (Dollar	1.4833	.6742
Europe (Euro)	1.0499	.95250
Germany (Mark)	2.054	.4869 (= 1/2.054)
Japan (Yen)	105.06	.009518
Mexico (Peso)	9.91	.100908

C. 1.23 (= [9.91 x 18,995]/ 152,100)
D. more; U.S.

2.
A. .75
B. demand; increase; increase
C. supply; increase; decrease
D. increase; supply; decrease
E. demand; increase; increase

3.

A. .25 (55,000 − 88,000e = 25,000 + 32,000e or 30,000 = 120,000e)

B. 25,636 (= 55,000 − 88,000 x .333); 35,656 (= 25,000 + 32,000 x .333)

C. greater than

D. 10,020 (= 35,656 − 25,636)

E. $3,340 (= 10,020 / 3)